THE THEORY OF GARMENT-PATTERN MAKING

A TEXTBOOK FOR CLOTHING DESIGNERS, TEACHERS OF CLOTHING TECHNOLOGY, AND SENIOR STUDENTS

BY

W. H. HULME

SOMETIME HEAD OF THE CLOTHING DEPARTMENT, LEEDS COLLEGE OF TECHNOLOGY LECTURER IN INDUSTRIAL HISTORY, DUDLEY AND STAFFORDSHIRE TECHNICAL COLLEGE

AUTHOR OF

THE ENGLISH TAILOR: A SHORT HISTORY OF THE TAILORING TRADE;

THE PRINCIPLES OF DRESS DESIGN, ETC.

British Library Cataloguing-in-Publication Data
A catalogue record for this book is available from the
British Library

Contents

Embroidery

Embroidery is the handicraft of decorating fabric or other materials with needle and thread or yarn. Embroidery may also incorporate other materials such as metal strips, pearls, beads, quills, and sequins. An interesting characteristic of embroidery is that the basic techniques or stitches on surviving examples of the earliest patterns —chain stitch, buttonhole or blanket stitch, running stitch, satin stitch, cross stitch—remain the fundamental techniques of hand embroidery today.

In *The Art of Embroidery,* written in 1964 by Marie Schuette and Sigrid Muller-Christensen, they noted the 'striking fact that in the development of embroidery ... there are no changes of materials or techniques which can be felt or interpreted as advances from a primitive to a later, more refined stage. On the other hand, we often find in early works a technical accomplishment and high standard of craftsmanship rarely attained in later times.' Embroidery has been dated to the Warring States period in China (5th-3rd century BC). The process used to tailor, patch, mend and reinforce cloth fostered the development of sewing techniques, and the decorative possibilities of sewing led to the art of embroidery. Embroidery was also a very important art in the Medieval Islamic world. One of the most interesting accounts of the craft has been given by the seventeenth century Turkish traveller, Evliya Çelebi, who called it the 'craft of the two hands.'

Because embroidery was a sign of high social status in Muslim societies, it became a hugely popular art. In cities such as Damascus, Cairo and Istanbul, embroidery was visible on handkerchiefs, uniforms, flags, horse trappings, slippers, sheaths, covers, and even on leather belts; often utilising gold and silver thread. It has since spread to the rest of the world, particularly the UK, where professional workshops and guilds garnered an immense reputation. The output of these workshops, called *Opus Anglicanum* or 'English work', was famous throughout Europe.

Embroidery can be classified according to whether the design is stitched *on top of* or *through* the foundation fabric, and by the relationship of stitch placement to the fabric. Several important classifications include 'free embroidery', where designs are applied without regard to the weave of the underlying fabric (such as traditional Chinese and Japanese embroidery), 'Counted Thread embroidery' where patterns are created by making stitches over a predetermined number of threads in the foundation fabric, and 'Canvas Work', where threads are stitched through a fabric mesh to create a dense pattern that completely covers the foundation fabric. This can be done on almost any fabric; wool, linen and silk have been in use for thousands of years, although today - cotton, ribbons, and organza are frequently utilised.

Whilst there is now a burgeoning market for commercial embroidery, and much contemporary embroidery is stitched with a computer using digital patterns, the art and pleasure of embroidery as a craft is making a comeback. We hope that the reader is inspired by this book to try some of their own!

FOREWORD

IN this volume I deal with the principles which underlie the making of garment patterns. A method of applying principles has for many years been called a "system" by designers in the various branches of the clothing trade. In the past the garment industry has not lacked systems: some of them have been based on the idea of human proportion—*i.e.*, they have been grounded in the size-card, which divides humans into types and sizes, differing from or approximating to accepted standards of physical proportion. Other systems are based on the unique requirements of the individual, human figure, having form and size peculiarly its own, and unrelated to all other forms.

The great garment industry, producing in bulk by factory methods, has been reared on the first point of view: the bespoke or merchant tailor bases his practice on the second.

This work deals only lightly with methods or systems: they rise and decline, and give place to others which take the making of a garment pattern a little nearer to certainty and finality. In a subsequent volume I shall deal with the systematic application of the basic principles stated here: in the present work I have set down the theory which lies behind all systems, and have treated measurement and its application in a fundamental way. The derivation of constructional scales and the application of scale quantites are dealt with in a new and clearer light: the pattern designer will thus be able to place his fitting points and arrange his garment parts with intelligence and confidence, and make his own system to his own requirements.

In the past, more emphasis has been laid on the mechanical application of principles by systems of pattern-making than on a clear understanding of the principles themselves. Nearly half-a-century spent in the retail and wholesale sections of the trade, and in teaching the technology of the industry, has convinced me of the need for a plain statement of the basic laws of human size and shape, and of their application to garment patterns. I make the assumption that these laws are a unity; that they apply to all garments and to both sexes. Size and shape exist in man, woman and child; in the old and the young; and all garments are subject to these major demands.

I wish to thank Alderman Elliott Young, Merchant Tailor, and Sidney Fryer, Director of Drescott Clothes, for reading over the manuscript and proofs and for making valuable suggestions.

W. H. H.

Dudley and Staffs. Technical College.

1944.

THE HUMAN BODY

"WHEN you employ persons to dress you, ask them, first, where on the body the measure ought to be placed, and to describe your figure as to carriage of involuntary form. If they cannot name and fix the anatomical points for measurement, nor intelligibly explain your figure, whether normal or abnormal in carriage, and in what parts, then they are deficient in the very preliminaries of the undertaking.

". . . it is evidently absurd to attempt to cover correctly even a simple form, as a cube, without a knowledge of it: and how much more absurd to attempt to dress or drape the human form correctly and tastefully without such knowledge" (Wampen, *Anthropometry*, III, 9–10).

The student of clothing should possess a good working knowledge of the parts of the body, the various types of figures, physical proportion, the effects of movement, and the relation of various fitting and draped garments to the body.

The Parts of the Body

As to the naming of the various parts of the body, no hard and fast rules may be imposed. Where a common name has, for any length of time, served to describe unmistakably any important physical feature it would be wise to retain and use it. For example, there is no good reason why the nape of the neck should be known by any other name; nor need the knee-cap, elbow and collar bone be described in Latin words. . Tradition should count for something in this matter; and so long as it is clearly understood by all concerned that certain names relate to certain parts of the body, no difficulty should arise.

There are, however, parts of the body which are of the first importance from the point of view of clothing, which have not yet acquired a fixed recognised English denomination and are referred to by all sorts of odd names. A good instance of this is the sternal notch, which has been called the "front-of-throat point", the "pit of the neck" and other clumsy terms. Again, there seems good reason why certain muscles of the upper arm and shoulder, often troublesome to the tailor, should be known as biceps, triceps, deltoids, etc.: there are no popular names one could use to describe them. The chief thing to be aimed at is definiteness; and whether the name of a part is that given to it by the anatomist, or whether it is an expressive term that has become generally accepted by usage, does not matter too much: what is important, however, is that teacher and student shall recognise the part concerned by the name that is used. This necessitates a common nomenclature, simple yet sufficient, and used in all theoretical and practical references. The object of this section, therefore, is to deal with the body and its parts, the skeleton and the muscles, and to give a working vocabulary. Every reference should be checked by the student with the plates and diagrams.

The Bone-Structure

The form of the body is determined by (1) the bony skeleton and (2) the overlying muscular system. The general configuration of the body is mainly determined by the bone-structure which supports the body vertically and gives rigidity to the trunk and limbs. In certain parts the bone-structure lies deep under the surface beneath a mass of muscular tissue—*e.g.*, the seat, where the massive gluteal muscles give to the part a shape different from that of the underlying bone-structure. In other parts the skeleton lies near to the surface and is merely overlaid by a thin layer of muscle. The shoulder (made up of the blades in rear, the upper ribs in front, and the collar bone) has its form mainly determined by these bones. "The muscles give the rounded and agreeable form to the human figure, but . . . they only give a finish to that form which the bones have originated. Taking the figure as a whole when covered with muscles, the rough outline is similar to that of the skeleton, though in detail, the corresponding parts are somewhat different." The form of the body, then, is determined by the bony skeleton and the muscles attached to it. These are subject to a number of influences which determine the attitude of the body, and which will be noted in their order.

The body may be divided under the following headings:—

(1) Head.	(2) Arms.
(3) Trunk.	(4) Legs.

When dealing with physical proportion it will be necessary to say something of the head: as a part of the body to be clothed, however, it has little interest for the tailor. The trunk of the body will claim our attention.

The spine, which supports the trunk, consists of small bones (vertebræ) which are so combined with each other that the whole spinal column is flexible. In the normal it describes a slight outward curve downwards from the nape, then inwards to the waist, and again slightly outwards below the waist.

The part of the spine connecting the trunk and the head contains seven vertebræ; the seventh, lowest and most prominent of these is the bone known as the nape of the neck, an important starting-point in pattern-drawing.

The second part, the dorsal vertebræ, are twelve in number, and lie between the nape and waist. The third, and lowest part, the lumbar vertebræ, five in number, connects with the large bone-structure of the loins, the pelvis. The vertebræ are largest in size in the lumbar region, less in the dorsal and smaller in the cervical. The spinal support of the trunk and head, then, is centrally situated in the back, very near to the surface of the body.

The bone-structure of the chest (thorax) comprises the ribs, which are joined to the spine at the back. The upper ribs are joined in front to the breast bone (sternum). The vital organs of the chest are protected by this bony cage of ribs.

In the back of the chest are the shoulder-blades (scapulae), the shape and position of which should be especially noted. Between the blades, in the centre of the back, is the middle hollow (median). The shape of the back, determined by the blades and the middle hollow, is of particular interest, in view of the problems of garment-fitting involved here. Its form, at rest and in movement, is of vital importance.

The end of the shoulder (the acromion of the blade), where the ball joint connects the upper arm with the blade and the collar bone, lies very near the surface of the body (as do all the larger joints), and thus directly influences the form.

The armpit (axilla) has no bone to locate its position. In view of their importance in the drawing of a pattern, the position of the following parts of the body should be specially fixed in the mind:—

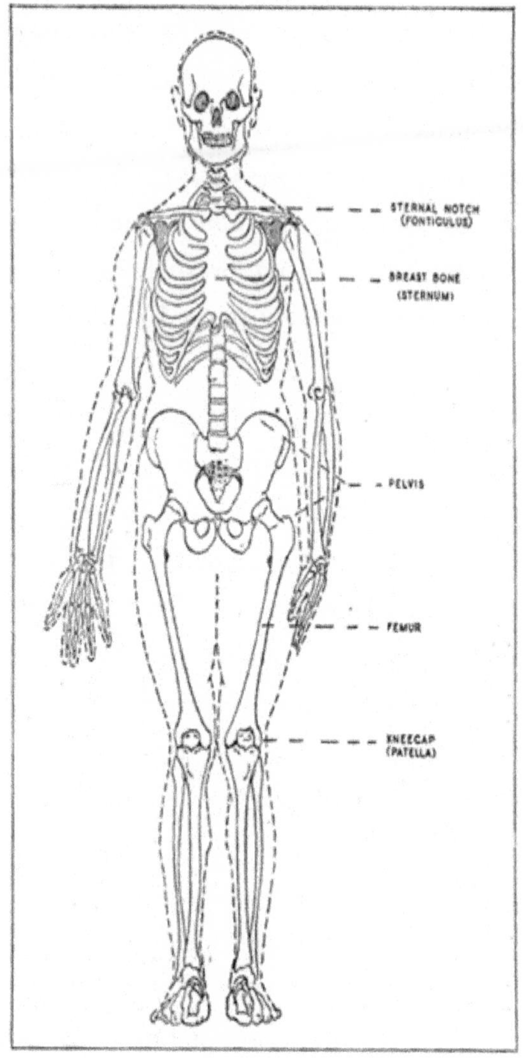

PLATE I.

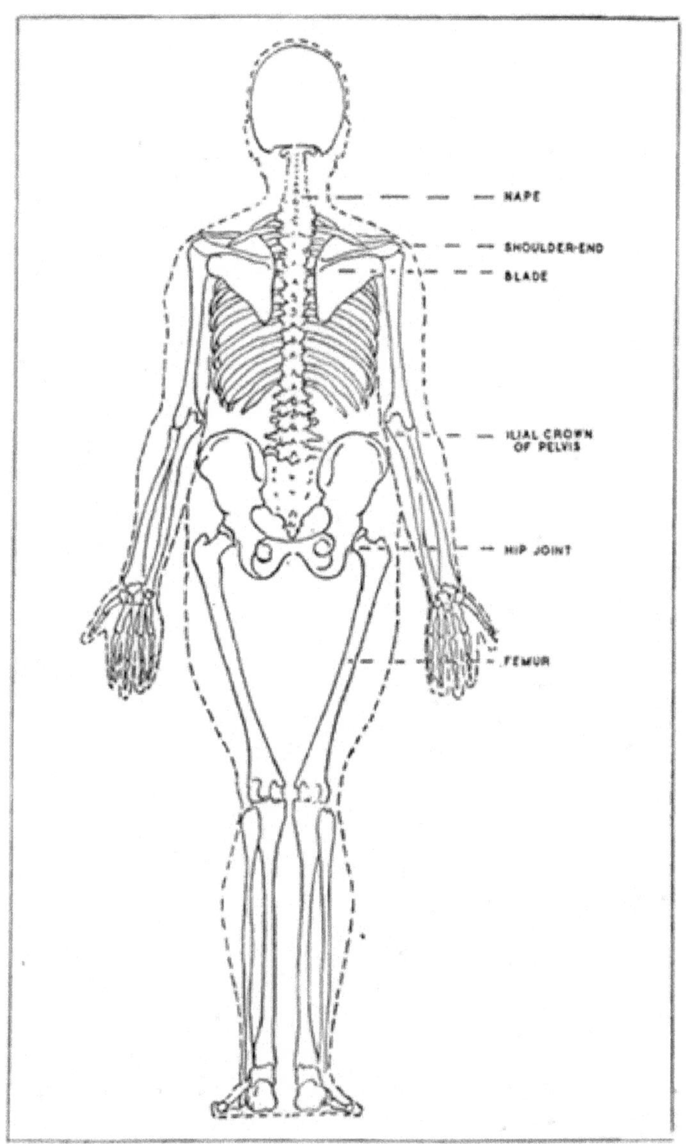
NAPE
SHOULDER-END
BLADE
ILIAL CROWN
OF PELVIS
HIP JOINT
FEMUR

PLATE II.

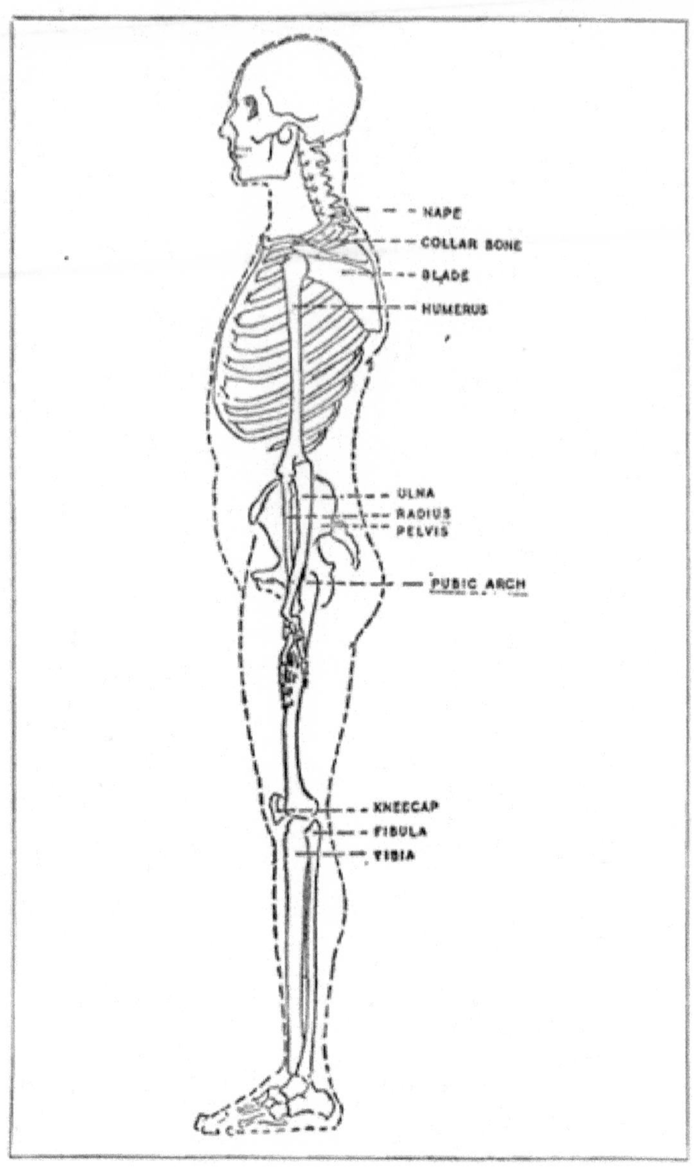
NAPE
COLLAR BONE
BLADE
HUMERUS
ULNA
RADIUS
PELVIS
PUBIC ARCH
KNEECAP
FIBULA
TIBIA

ATE III.

the nape (seventh cervical vertebræ),
the fonticulus (sternal notch),
the shoulder blades (scapulae),
the acromion of the blade (shoulder end),
the armpit (axilla),
the ilial points (crown of the pelvis),
the knee-cap (patella).

The Muscular System and its Types of Development

The muscles, as the final determinant of shape or form, should be carefully studied from this point of view. Over- or underdevelopment of any, or all, of the muscles will have a very decisive effect on physical shape. The following muscles are so intimately connected with the correct fitting of clothing, that their position, and possible development, should be especially noted:—

the trapezius (the neck),
the deltoids (arm and shoulder),
the greater pectoral (chest),
the latissimus dorsi (the lower blade),
the gluteal group (the seat),

the vastus externus (the outer thigh),
the gastrocnemius (the calf).

"It is a well-known truth that, through motion and exertion, physical as well as mental powers are developed; and therefore it may truly be inferred that exercise has an especial influence over the muscles, the effect of which is to strengthen them, and in undergoing such a change they also become larger. The reverse of this is likewise equally true: where there is neither motion nor exertion there is no development, and, as a natural consequence, neither increase nor strength to be expected, but that rather the muscles may become diminished and weakened.

"Through certain circumstances it may happen that some muscles on the human body become developed at the same time that others remain undeveloped. This occurs in cases where the occupation of the person is such as to occasion too great relaxation in these muscles, while the others are in much action and exertion.

"The muscles partly fix the form of the human figure; and, further, as an irregular or unequal development of them is detrimental and even destructive to its normal form, it follows that we may partly conclude from the occupation of the person his especial form of figure.

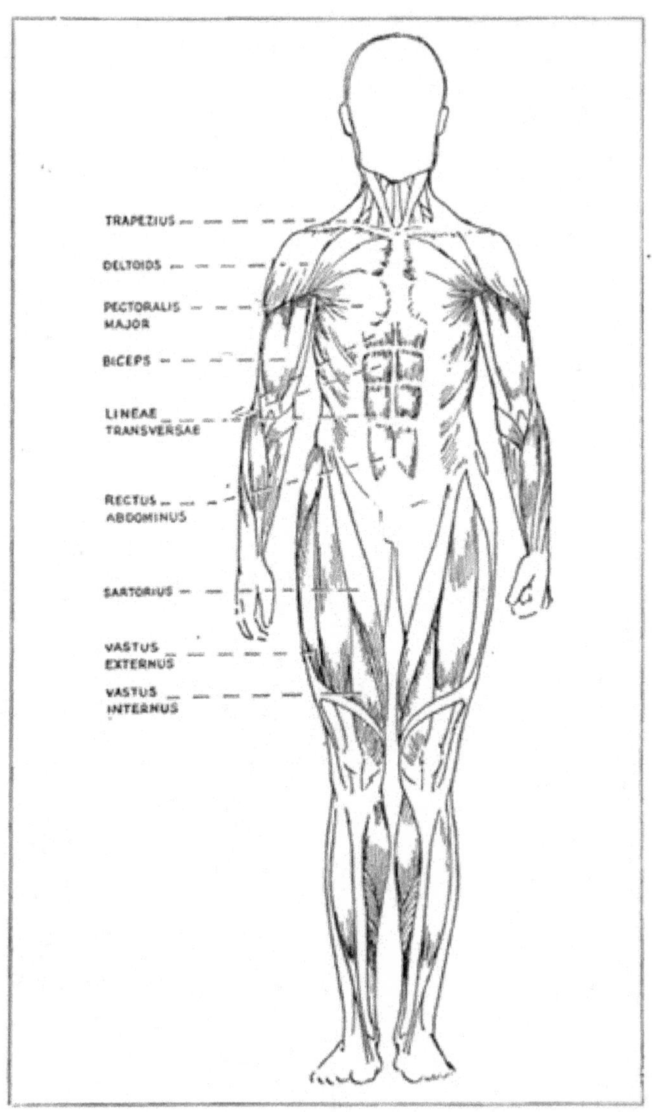
TRAPEZIUS
DELTOIDS
PECTORALIS MAJOR
BICEPS
LINEAE TRANSVERSAE
RECTUS ABDOMINUS
SARTORIUS
VASTUS EXTERNUS
VASTUS INTERNUS

PLATE IV.

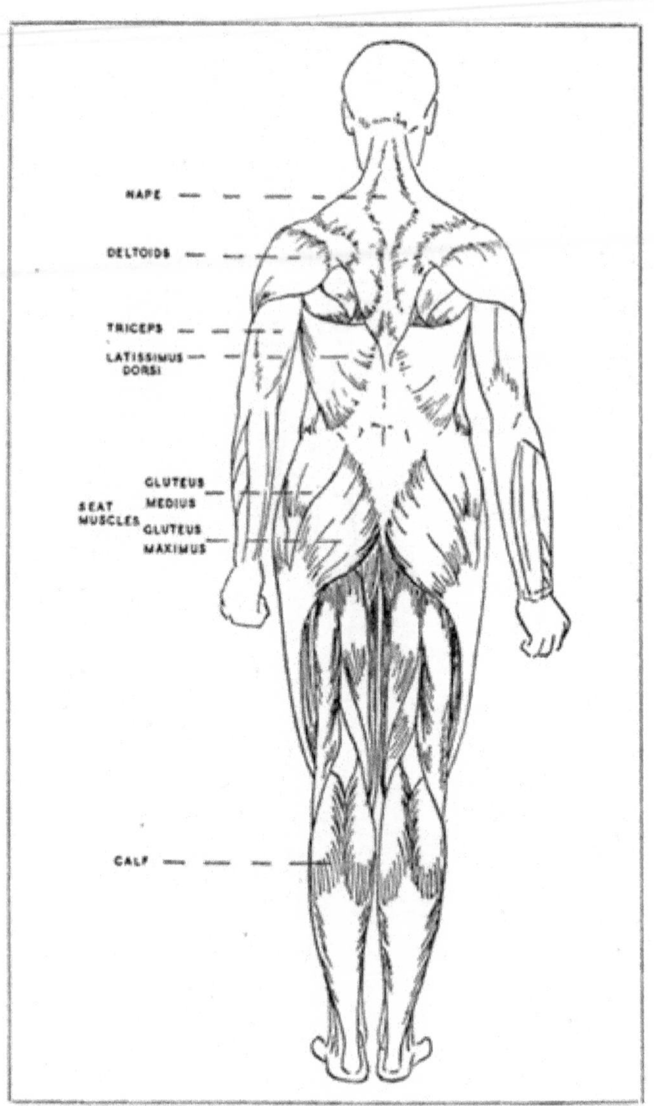
NAPE
DELTOIDS
TRICEPS
LATISSIMUS DORSI
SEAT MUSCLES
GLUTEUS MEDIUS
GLUTEUS MAXIMUS
CALF

PLATE V.

"Before we define the form of the figure in its details, it must be borne in mind that by a uniform development of the muscles as a whole the normal form of the figure is not disturbed, whether their development is in a great or in a small degree; because, through the increase or decrease of the parts, the form of the figure does not alter, as they retain, by such uniformity of development to each other, their proportions. Hence, when we obtain a large measure, from a figure highly developed in muscle, we may certainly conclude that all parts of the figure stand in a normal ratio to this measure; and it is precisely the same in obtaining a small measure from a figure wherein the muscles are sparingly developed.

"Bearing these considerations in mind, it will be seen which of the muscles develop themselves simultaneously and which are developed singly, while others in the same time remain undeveloped. This can easily be done by observing persons in their occupation. For instance, in the case of an orator or a soldier, or in those who have undergone gymnastic exercises, the pectoralis and deltoid muscles are considerably developed; hence these persons are full in the chest and shoulder, the former being large in relation to the back; and the trapezius and latissimus dorsi muscles are only slightly developed, unless when well regulated by gymnastic exercises. Opposition to this, in the habitually indolent, the pectoralis muscle only is tolerably developed.

"In such persons the chest is in abnormal ratio to the back; because the surface of the chest is, in proportion, much greater to the surface of the back than the normal ratio between these two surfaces admits—occasioned more by an assumption of a stately deportment than by any development of the muscles.

"On the other hand, in the industrious class—as, for instance, those whose occupation is laborious—the latissimus dorsi, the trapezius, the levator scapulæ, the deltoids, the infra spinatus, and the teres muscles are highly developed, and the pectoralis as much retarded; hence these persons are thick in the neck, broad in the back, and round in the shoulders. In these the chest surface is again in abnormal ratio to the surface of the back, because the former is less to the back than the normal ratio demands.

"With regard to those persons whose occupation is light and requires stooping, as, for instance, in that of literature or writing, the above-named muscles are all only slightly developed; but their form is somewhat similar to that of the artisan, and a common sign between them of industry. This last-mentioned weak form falls principally to the learned professionalist, and artist, in whom also the chest is in abnormal ratio to the back, because it is again smaller to the back than the normal ratio allows. But generally this abnormal difference is not very considerable, and may therefore be in most cases removed by gymnastic exercise; especially as it rarely happens among this class that an irregular development of muscle exists to cause the abnormal form in the figure, it really lying, as will soon be seen, in the position of the bones.

"If we obtain a measure from a figure whose muscular development causes abnormality in the form, it may certainly be concluded that the parts of it stand in abnormal ratio to that measure." (Wampen, *Anatomy*, p. 3.)

Every activity, then, either of recreation or occupation, influences the shape of the body in some locality and to some extent. When labour was more manual and less mechanical than now, occupational causes were responsible for many more well-recognised physical effects.

With the passing of the blacksmith's trade will pass the "brawny arm" development of the smith. The strenuousness of labour-tasks has, during recent years, been softened, and the hard manual work that produced pronounced physical types has been displaced by mechanical labour-saving devices. The excavator to-day is not often a man, but very frequently a machine. "Brawn" is not demanded or developed as it formerly was. Industry no longer produces the pronounced physical types to anything like the same extent. On the other hand, the soft-handed occupations are manned by a physically better type. Few indoor workers there are who do not take pleasure from some form of outdoor physical exercise or game. Thus the old physical differences which undoubtedly existed between the two types of worker no longer hold good to the same degree. The toiler toils less hardly; the soft-handed worker plays more strenuously. From each side there is some approximation to a physical norm, and a greater degree of figure standardisation has become possible. There are fewer exceptions than formerly to any physical rule. It is possible, therefore, to include, within one or other of the recognised form-types of the wholesale clothing trade, a larger number of the male population than formerly.

When these things have been said, however, it is still true that any occupation demanding the abnormal use of any particular set of muscles will produce a characteristic physical form. This is also true of occupations in which workers must habitually assume certain attitudes which tend to become permanent. The slight forward stoop, the dropped shoulder, the head-forward posture known as the "students' stoop", are all physical reflections of occupational attitudes.

Many of the larger firms doing a special order trade have made a practice of asking that the occupation of the customer be included among the data set out on the order form.

PHYSICAL PROPORTIONS

THE relation of the various parts of the body to each other, in the proportionate, or regular, figure and in other recognised form types, should be regarded as a necessary study by the garment-designer.

In thinking over the previous notes on the parts and structure of the body one is impressed by *the sense of unity and harmony which characterises the normal form*. The body should not be regarded as a haphazard assemblage of unrelated parts. Just as the various organs of the trunk and head are functionally related and inter-dependent, so all the parts of the body combine to form a harmonious entity possessing qualities of form and size which must be understood in their relation to clothing.

Definitions

Proportion.—Comparative relation; derived from the phrase proportione = for, or in respect of (his or its) share. A portion or part, in its relation to the whole. Due relation of one part to another: such relation of size, etc., between things or parts of a thing, as renders the whole harmonious. Balance, symmetry, agreement, harmony.

Generally: a body may be said to be proportionate when its various parts are in relative harmony with each other. Particularly: agreement, or harmony, of the relative lengths and girths of its parts.

Disproportion.—Generally: out of proportion, having no due relation in size, amount, etc. Particularly: disagreement or lack of harmony of the lengths and girths of parts of the body.

Normal.—Conforming to a standard or type. Regular, natural, usual. When speaking of a normal figure we mean a typical person who has no unusual features.

Abnormal.—Deviating from a standard or type. Irregular, excessive, unusual—*e.g.*, abnormal shoulder development = shoulder excessively developed; abnormally stout = corpulency, excessive stoutness.

Subnormal.—Less than normal; undeveloped.

Average Dimensions.—The *mean* of any number of sets of dimensions—*e.g.*, the average breast measure of five men, measuring respectively 34 ins., 35 ins., 37 ins., 39 ins., 40 ins., is 37 ins.

The average height of British troops during the Great War was stated to be 5 ft. 8 ins.

Symmetry.—"This is a quality which everyone understands to be in a form taken as a whole, where all corresponding parts, each to each, are equal in dimension and similar or alike in position; as, for instance, in the human form are two equal arms, two eyes of equal size and at equal distance each to each, etc.: such is always the quality of the involuntary form if it is normal" (Wampen, *Anthro.*, p. 46).

Deformity.—Want of proper form or symmetry; unnatural shape or form; irregularity of shape. Particularly, malformation of the bone structure of the body—*e.g.*, hunch back, pigeon chest, bow and K legs.

Form.—Shape, configuration; the visible aspect of a thing. The particular character, outline or structure of a thing. The shape and structure of anything as distinguished from the material of which it is composed. The particular disposition of matter, giving it individuality or distinctive character.

Physical form = the shape of the body.

Shape.—Set form.

Size.—A fixed quantity; magnitude; extent of volume or surface, dimensions of a figure.

Growth.—To extend, to become greater in any way, to increase in size.

Development.—A gradual unfolding; a growth along normal and expected lines.

Where growth of the body may mean the mere deposit of tissue, development implies an advance towards maturity of shape or form.

Fitting Garment.—A garment, or part of a garment, may be said to fit the body when the garment, or the part, follows closely the contours of the body—*e.g.*, a waistcoat, fitting the body at all points, is a fitting garment.

Draped Garment.—A garment may be said to be draped when material in excess of the body's minimum requirements is introduced—*e.g.*, a normal pair of trousers may be regarded as fitting in the trunk portion, but draped in the legs.

Pattern.—A garment pattern is a full-size replica of the garment for which it is cut. There will be as many parts of the pattern as there are parts of the garment. Seams (or turnings) and inlays and upturns, may, or may not, be included in the pattern.

Construction Lines.—Measurements are taken on certain lines on the body. The construction lines reproduce, on the drawing, the lines on which the measurements were taken on the body. They should be regarded as the girder work of pattern construction and as a means by which the measurements are correctly transferred to the pattern.

With these terms defined as they affect clothing, we go on to the proportions of the normal regular figure.

1. Partial Height Related to Total Height: Men.

The length of the head has for centuries been the accepted unit of physical height. The total height is computed at 7 3/4 heads; almost one half (actually 3 3/4 heads) is the length of the head and trunk; slightly more than one half (actually 4 heads) represents the leg length.

Trunk.

Armpit to the wrist bone = 2 heads.

Nape, down the spine, to the waist = 2 heads.

Nape to the level of the armpits = 1 head.

Fork to the waist = 1 head plus 2 ins.

Sitting height = about 53 per cent. of total stature.

Leg.

Ankle to the (top of) knee-cap = about 54 per cent. of leg length (ankle to fork).

The pubic arch is equidistant from crown and sole.

The following three height quantities will be found of approximate equal amount:—

Ilial crown to knee-cap.

Knee-cap to ground.

Acromion of scapula to pubic arch.

2. Girths Related to Each Other: Men.

Trunk.

Neck girth = about 40 per cent. of breast girth.

Seat girth = about 7 per cent. more than breast girth.

Waist girth (a very variable relative dimension) = 85 to 90 per cent. of breast girth.

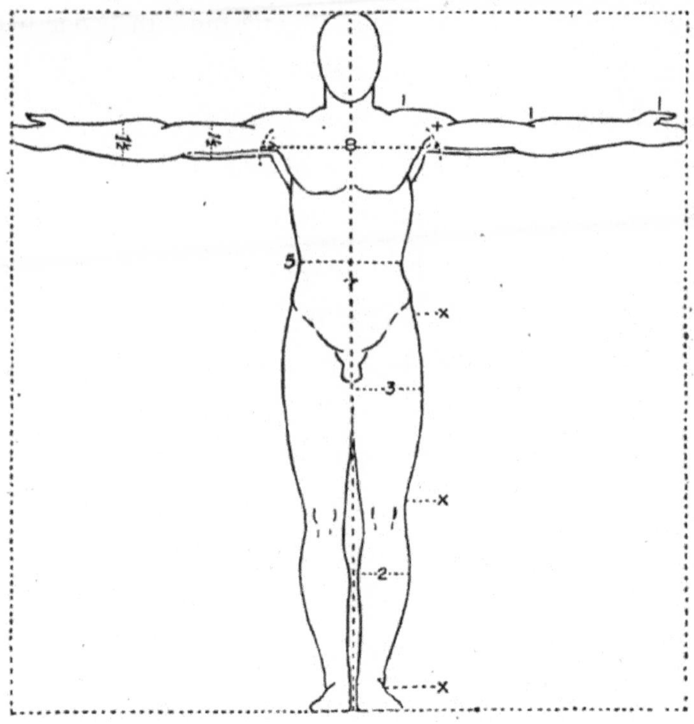

FIG. 1.

3. Height Related to Girth and Breadth.

"It is a popular assertion that one's span is equal to one's stature. This is nearly true, *on the average*." The many exceptions, however, to this general statement render the comparison unreliable.

4. The relation of the middle shoulder measurement to the breast girth is, in the proportionate form of normal development, as 3 : 4. A comparison of these two important measurements will at once give the shoulder development

relative to the breast girth. If the data are accurately taken, the height, breast girth, and middle shoulder measure, treated comparatively, will go far to assess and place the form type.

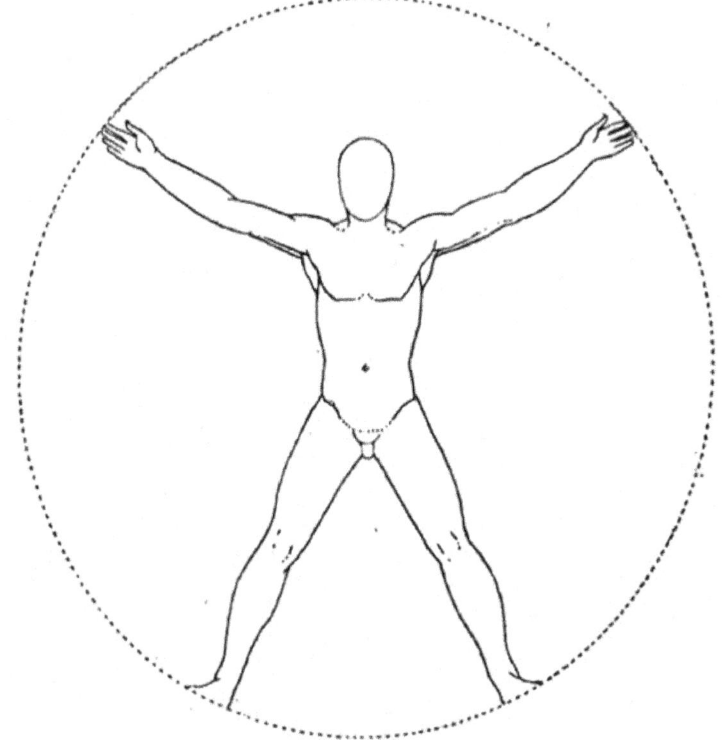

FIG. 2.

The Body Rise: Men

This quantity is the distance from the fork line to the waist line. It does not concern that part of the trousers *above* the *waist* line, and takes no account of the top band.

In cases where direct measures of side and inside leg are used, the amount of body rise is readily found by deducting the inside leg measurement from the side.

Example.

Side measurement	42 ins.
Inside leg	31 1/2 ins.
	⊠
Body rise	10 1/2 ins.

Where, however, stock garments are to be designed, a formula giving directions for ascertaining the body rise will be desirable.

Formula.

$$\text{Body rise} = \frac{\text{height}}{8} \text{ plus 2 ins.}$$

This formula may be applied to all leg garments for proportionate form types. The student is warned that it should not be used for leg garments for figures of abnormal development—*e.g.*, corpulent.

Clearly, the distance between the fork and the waist is part of the total height of a man. If the total height is greater than normal, the amount of body rise will be abnormal.

Where the height is below normal, the amount of body rise will be subnormal. The part varies proportionately to the whole. The point to grasp is that the quantity should be related to the height of the man.

A standard height with its proportionate body rise should be established, in respect of which additions or subtractions may be made.

Every inch more or less of height will, then, reflect 1/8 in. plus or minus in the body rise.

Standard.

Height: 5 ft. 8 ins. = 10 1/2 ins. body rise.

Method.

Add or deduct 1/8 in. of body rise for every inch of height in excess of, or less than, the standard height of 5 ft. 8 ins.

Examples.

Height: 5 ft. 5 ins. (minus 3/8 in.) = 10 1/8 ins. body rise.

Height: 5 ft. 11 ins. (plus 3/8 in.) = 10 7/8 ins. body rise.

Height: 6 ft. 3 ins. (plus 7/8 in.) = 11 3/8 ins. body rise.

Where a waist-band is attached to the top side, the amount necessary for one seam should be left over the above quantities. A seam should also be added to the lower edge of the waist-band.

Growth and Development

By *growth* of the body is meant the putting on of tissue in a more or less even way; that every increase in size is fairly constant in all parts.

By *development* is implied an increase in size; not an even deposit of that increase, but rather an addition to the size and weight of the body that takes the form of local increases of various kinds. When speaking of a "growing boy" we have chiefly in mind the putting-on of weight; when a maid is described as "developing into womanhood", something more than a mere increase in weight is indicated;

what is rather stressed is the gradual assumption of the form characteristic of the fully-developed woman.

Each successive stage of life has its characteristic physical form possessing certain distinguishing notes. In one stage growth will be general; in others development of form, or distinctive shape, will be the dominant note. The form may even change while the weight remains hardly altered. Up to early manhood the bone structure is growing and hardening; in the later years the changes in form are due to loss or increase of tissue or to lesions in the controls of the skeleton.

Were growth from birth general, and all parts of the body grew at exactly the same rate, the adult male would have the form of the infant with the size of the man. At birth the length of the head is about one-quarter of the total length of the body, and at five years, one-sixth; at the age of nine years the head measures into the height about six-and-a-half times; at adult stature, nearly eight times. The trunk and limbs therefore increase in length by nearly twice the amount that the head lengthens between infancy and manhood.

Again, in the early years sitting height is a larger part of standing height than in adult manhood. The legs, therefore, increase in length at a slightly greater rate than do the trunk and head combined. The lengthening of the arms keeps fairly equal to the growth of the legs.

Further, in infancy and young boyhood a comparison of the three chief trunk girths—breast, waist, and seat—shows a virtual equality. This shape of trunk may be again reached later in life, the short, stout figure being similar in *shape*, while being much larger in *size*.

Growth, then, is not regular and even, but sporadic and local. At one period length growth will be more marked than girth increase; at another, girth will develop after length increase has ceased. Or, again, one girth may increase while others remain almost stationary, thus altering the relative proportions of the body and giving a different form. These continual modifications in the size and shape of the body determine the characteristic figure at any given stage of life.

When it is considered that the growth and development of the body are continually being conditioned by many factors, from hereditary influences to the kind of food consumed, the occupation followed, and the games played, it is remarkable that so large a percentage of the male population falls within the range of sizes shown on the normal size card. And although the number of intermediate "fittings" has grown in recent years, they should be understood as being related to varieties of style and fabric and only to a less extent slight modifications of recognised sizes.

From Cradle to Grave

1. The small boy's trunk is thick and almost cylindrical. His posture is very erect and, when standing, the feet are usually farther apart than during the succeeding stage of development. The arms and legs are thick, and, relative to trunk length, shorter than a few years later.

2. From the age of about ten years it will be noted that the girth of the waist does not increase as do the breast and seat measurements. The boy begins to "shoot up", as the phrase goes, and to generally take on something of the adult figure. He loses the stocky build of the earlier stage and, with it, the erectness of posture. He is leaving the characteristic shape of the small boy behind, and every year sees a nearer approximation to the man's stature and form. From about the age of fifteen years this development is more marked and noticeable than at any other period of life.

3. Full stature is reached probably between twenty and twenty-four: little, if any, height increase takes place after this age. The body as a whole has by now taken on its characteristic adult form, whether tall, average or short, stocky or sparely-built. The only changes which may take place are in girth and posture.

4. Some few men are fortunately exempt from the thickening of the body which is a definite characteristic of the middle years of life, and retain, until well on into

middle age, the more slender build of early manhood. The majority, however, increase in weight and become stocky. Some, indeed, become corpulent and have the erect attitude and open-legged stance associated with corpulency. Occupational causes, diet and other habits, and the amount of physical exercise obtainable will largely determine the physical characteristics of middle life.

5. In advanced age there is a slight contraction of the framework of the body, resulting in a shrinkage of the bone and tissue, and in an increasingly stooping posture.

Thus at every period of life the body has its own peculiar characteristics; and although any attempt to group these round certain ages, or to designate sizes by age, will prove unsatisfactory, it is still true that a knowledge of the growth and development of the body should be possessed by the student.

Recognised Form Types

The size card of wholesale clothing firms is an elaboration of an early and simple grouping of forms. Wampen analysed three main types of figure and showed the sub-types related to each.

His main divisions were:—

(*a*) the proportionate form $h = b$,

(*b*) the slender form $h > b$,

(*c*) the broad form $h < b$.

Two varieties of (*c*), the broad form, are the short stout, and the stout.

An impression of any type of figure may be conveyed by words, by figures, or by illustration. Most of the trade technical journals regularly publish photographic illustrations of garments in wear; and the variety of figures shown will enable the student to be familiar with the outlines and general appearance of the various form types. Impressions of length, or girth, or shortness, or some peculiarity of posture will become associated in the mind with certain types of figure. Thus a very general impression of what is meant by a regular, or a stout, is formed.

This general impression may be amplified by the study of a size card giving the main dimensions. In this way a more exact impression is formed. If two different sets of dimensions are compared and points of similarity and of difference are developed and expressed in numbers, more has been learned than if distinguishing features of the two figures had been noted without a comparison being made.

If a table of detailed proportionate quantities is studied, a large number of sectional dimensions relating to one size will indicate the shape and posture, as well as the size of the figure.

The Regular Figure

The outstanding characteristic of this form type is that it is proportionate. There is a harmony of height and girth in all sizes; and the various girth measurements are also in harmonious proportion to each other.

The regular figure is found in a wide range of sizes: indeed, size can exist independent of a sense of proportion. A regular figure may be 5 ft. 6 ins. height, or 5 ft. 11 ins., but so long as the girths accord with the height, the form is proportionate or regular. The relation of girth to height can best be visualised by reference to the size card of regular sizes. It will be noted that in all sizes the girths maintain an approximate ratio and that every increase in girth assumes a proportionate increase in height. Thus in this range of sizes, whether the figure is 34 ins. breast or 42 ins. there is an approximate proportionate relationship between the various girths and also between the breast girth and the height.

This constancy of dimensional relationship in all sizes assumes a standard regular figure near average size, and the clothing industry has adopted a physical standard which embodies the idea of proportion.

**Standard: Height, 5 ft. 8 ins.
Nape to waist, 17 ins.
In sleeve 18 ins.
In leg (P.B.), 32 ins.** } **lengths.**

**Breast, 38 ins.
Waist, 34 ins.
Seat, 40 ins.** } **girths.**

This standard gives a definite relationship of the various measures to each other. The ratios will remain approximately constant even when the sizes are greater or less than the standard.

For example, the ratio of breast to seat is as 38 is to 40, and the ratio will be fairly constant in all sizes.

The ratio of height to breast girth is as 68 is to 38, and this ratio will remain constant in all sizes.

It is, therefore, plain that the dominant characteristic of the regular figure is the sense of physical proportion which is common to all sizes. The sizes vary from 33 ins. to 44 ins. breast girth with corresponding heights, but all the sizes are approximately proportionate.

The posture, or attitude, of the regular figure is assumed to be normally upright; not stooping in any marked degree nor over-erect. The principles of garment balance are involved here, and it should be definitely understood that every sectional system of pattern-drawing assumes this normally erect attitude of the regular figure. Thus the system laid down should be regarded as providing for the balance requirements of the regular figure. Any provision for over-erectness or for stooping will be made outside of the normal working of the system.

The Long Figure

The chief characteristic of the long form type is that the height of the figure is greater in relation to the girths than in the regular form. The standard long figure of 38 ins. breast girth would be 6 ft. in height. Compared with the standard regular form, the long is taller than proportionate having regard to the girths; the figure may, therefore, be regarded as disproportionate.

The first thing that strikes the observer is the height of the figure.

A closer comparison of the size-card dimensions of the long sizes with the regular forms will show that *all* height quantities will be greater. If the height standard of the long size is calculated at, say, 4 ins. more than the regular, this amount must be allocated, in correct proportion, to the various parts of the garments. The leg measure will be greater than the regular by about 2 ins., the leg being about half of the total height. The nape to waist will be reckoned as about a quarter of the height, and will therefore be increased by 1 in. The insleeve will be lengthened by a similar amount; and the scye will need to be about 1/2 in. deeper than the regular of the same breast girth. The body rise of the trousers and the full length of the vest will also need proportionate increase.

A further point to note, when comparing the long with the regular sizes, is that the long type is usually rather sparely built. This is seen in the waist girth, which is slightly smaller in the long than in the regular sizes.

The attitude, too, is somewhat different; the tall man is not quite so erect as the regular type. This slight difference in posture requires a slightly longer back balance and a shorter front balance length. A slight forward movement of the front neck point may also be needed.

The Short Figure

The chief characteristic of the short figure is that the height is less than expected having regard to the girths. The standard short figure of 38 ins. breast girth would be about 5 ft. 4 ins. in height. The figure is, therefore, disproportionate.

Compared with similar breast girths of the regular figure, the waist girths of the short figure will be found slightly greater.

The attitude of the short figure is usually a little more erect than the regular, and certainly more erect than the long type. This difference in posture will affect the balance lengths, the back requiring to be a little shorter than the regular, and the front a little longer. The front neck point may need moving slightly backward to allow for this posture.

The Stout Figure

The height factor in the stout figure is that of the regular figure of the same breast girth. The distinctive features are the excess of girth and a general stockiness of build. The trunk girths nearly approximate, suggesting a more or less cylindrical form.

The attitude is usually erect, and balance adjustment should be made on this account.

The Short-Stout Figure

This form type stands to the short figure as does the stout to the regular. The general stockiness of build and erectness of posture are, of course, similar to those of the stout figure. This type is more frequent in the thickly populated industrial areas of the provinces and among men in middle life.

The Corpulent Figure

A man is said to be corpulent when his waist girth is greater than the breast girth. It is, of course, a fairly common form of disproportion, and the degree of disproportion is seen by comparing the actual waist girth with a proportionate waist girth. For example, the proportionate waist measurement of a man of 42 ins. breast girth would be 38 1/2 ins., if he were actually 46 ins. waist measurement the disproportion would amount to 10 ins.

Not every large man is corpulent: a man may be dimensionally large but quite proportionately built. This note is made here in view of a rather common error in confusing large size with disproportion; in deriving constructional scales a confusion of the two-form types may result in wrong quantities and in the incorrect placing of parts.

Most corpulent men of normal habit stand very erect: the deposit of an abnormal amount of tissue on the front of the body and the consequent necessity of maintaining a physical balance will account for this erectness. The feet are usually wider apart when standing than is usual with men of slender or regular build. These characteristics in the body must be reproduced in the garments, and the longer front and shorter back-balance in the trunk garments, and the openness of leg-construction in the leg garments will secure good fitting.

The Female Form Compared with the Male Figure

The description of the male structure will apply, with certain important qualifications, to the female form. The skeleton framework and its covering muscular tissue are substantially the same; but the male skeleton is larger and stronger, both in total and in parts; while the two bodies compared show a smaller, lighter, smoother, softer female form, more graceful in its lines and contours.

The many *small* local differences in form and proportion may be an interesting study to the anatomist, but will have no great attraction for the garment designer. Only those differences in size, proportion, and shape which directly affect the garment pattern will concern us here.

(1) The average woman is less in height than the average man. On the figures available, the nearest estimate will give a difference of 3 1/2 to 4 ins. shorter.

(2) Basing the height of the proportionate woman on 7 3/4 heads, 4 heads will be taken up by head and trunk, 3 3/4 by the legs. In the male this ratio is reversed. In terms of the human figure these proportions mean that the legs are both actually and relatively shorter, and the body relatively longer, than in the male. This extra trunk length is not spread evenly over the length of the torso, but is found entirely in the height of the pelvic structure—*i.e.*, the fork-to-waist section, the body rise.

This greater ratio of trunk length to leg length may be seen in the similarity of the sitting height of men and women. Seated at dinner, all would seem about the same height; standing, however, they reveal the shorter leg length of women.

(3) A corollary of (2) is the relatively wider pelvic structure of the female. This gives, on the two dimensions, a large pelvic region compared with the male; and may be regarded as Nature's provision for child-bearing.

(4) The shoulder-mass is less bulky in size and more graceful in shape; due to less development of the muscles over bones that are smaller.

(5) The waist is more slender; and this slenderness is accentuated by the greater lateral spread of the hips. The hips and thigh are proportionately larger.

(6) The arm socket (scye) is smaller than in the male, and is placed slightly higher in the trunk.

(7) The neck is longer, and the shoulders more erect, the nape of neck being in the *W* size of normal posture, about 1 1/4 ins. in from a vertical line, as compared with 2 1/2 ins. in the regular man's figure of normal stance. (8) The bust, a purely local development of the mammary glands, varies in size at different stages of physical development and experience. In the average *W.* figure it may be placed at 2 1/2 to 3 ins. over the breast dimension. Its position will vary with its size. Very heavy bust development will be found, in the unclothed body, very near to the waist line. Corsetry, however, lifts and controls such excessive development.

Growth and Development

The growth and development of the girl into the woman follow the same phases as in the boy developing into manhood.

There are similar periods of bone lengthening, of tissue deposit, of bust development: slow and gradual changes which, in sum total and over years, result in the characteristic form of the adult woman.

The *standard* of the mantle trade is a figure of complete development, about 65 ins. height, 38 ins. bust, 35 1/2 ins. breast, 42 ins. hips. This standard is designated *W*, and forms a standard to which all other sizes and figures are compared.

Just as in the forms of men there are variations of height, giving a variety of greater or less lengths to almost identical girths. These may be regarded as the longs and shorts of the mantle trade. Variations of girth give the matron's and outsizes, corresponding to the stouts and short stouts.

All these different forms are reflected in the size cards, and practically every variety of female form can be fitted. The keen student can, by a study of a good scale of sizes, trace the growth of the girl and her gradual development into womanhood. A good class or homework exercise would be a word description of one of the various sizes which, on the size card, is indicated by numeral only.

The number of abnormalities in women is less than in men. True, there are figures who stoop a little; others who are too erect to be entirely graceful. There are, too, the X sizes, denoting larger hip girth in an otherwise normal figure. It has been argued that "women conform in a greater degree to the ideal form than do men"; and it seems to be true, for a larger percentage of women can be fitted from stock sizes than is the case with men.

In the section on scale-finding, attention is drawn to the differences in size due to underclothing and differences in shape due to corsetry. The point must be made here, in advance, that while women's underclothes are nowadays lighter and less bulky than men's, yet even the most modern brassiere does produce a form which, in its controlled modelling, differs from the nude, natural figure. Fashion demands, and conventional corsetry gives, a flat front abdominal wall; yet in the nude figure it is not so flat. Corsetry affects not only the shape of the torso, but also, by compression and control, its relative dimensions.

The student should be acquainted with the tables of nude proportions which have been drawn up by the anthropometrists, but he should interpret them in the light of any changes made by corsetry and undies.

Disproportionate Fashion Drawings

There arises here a practical consideration with regard to fashion drawings which may be seen in advertisements, and in dress journals which are eagerly bought by women, which convey an entirely false impression of the figure and, therefore, of the garment depicted. It appears to be the object of many fashion artists to endow their figures with those physical proportions desired by many women but possessed by none. Even then, they exaggerate the desirable into the freakish.

To draw a figure with a slightly longer waist-to-foot length than Nature has given, is pardonable. To produce a figure 10 heads in height, with the extra 2 heads given to leg length is absurd. Nor do the girths agree with the height. If the girths are those of, say, *W* size, then the drawing suggests a height of 7 feet. If the height is that of even a tall woman, the girths would be those of a size 6. To attempt to reproduce, in a garment for a normal woman, the proportions of these drawings is to attempt the impossible. Yet women persist in bringing them to be copied in terms of cloth and trimmings.

Every student will collect illustrations of figure types and garment styles; they will help him in his studies. But they should be true representations of what is intended. The movement away from line drawings and towards photographs will have been observed during recent years. The advice is, therefore, collect good photographs from good-class fashion journals.

THE SIZING OF GARMENTS

A NUMBER of documents are appended, which cover the recent British and American work in the standardisation of garment sizes. The origin is indicated in each case, and they have been selected from many similar size charts for reasons which will be obvious. Where antecedent circumstances were necessary to a clear understanding, these have been stated.

The Idea of Size Notation

The making of clothing to standard sizes is not a new idea. In the seventeenth century tailors in busy ports—*e.g.*, Bristol—kept a stock of clothing of standard sizes for those of their maritime customers who had not the time in port to wait for the finishing of a bespoke garment. This, however, was exceptional: the normal way was to be measured, and to wait the tailor's pleasure.

It was not until a century ago that ready-to-wear clothing, of stock size, began to sell in quantity. No size notation was then in use. In the fifties and sixties of last century the first of our modern clothing firms were founded, and "off-the-peg" garments began to be made in bulk. The poorer folk were better clothed; but the rest of the world frowned on "reach-me-downs". Men's suits were, at this time, sized by a number, denoting an approximate set of girth measured. Size 3 was a nominal 34 breast, 4 was 36, 5 was a 38, and 6 was 40-in. breast. The size range was very limited: shape was scarcely attempted.

This notation of sizes remained in use until fairly recently; indeed, it outstayed its usefulness by many years. Size numbers ceased to have any exact size meaning; each manufacturer put his own close or easy interpretation on the figures to a degree that rendered absurd any code of sizes. It was only after the clothing manufacturers realised that the feeble attempts at size standardisation had simply broken down that a move was made towards the size notation in use today.

The Executive Council of the Wholesale Clothing Manufacturers' Federation of Great Britain appointed a special committee to deal with the question of sizing. The following recommendations based on the committee's findings were issued to members:—

RECOMMENDATION TO MEMBERS *RE* MARKING OF SIZES

1. Suits, Overcoats, etc.

It is recommended that the *breast measure* on the ticket be regarded as the size in substitution for the numeral at present in use, for example:

(*a*) A man's lounge suit, overcoat, or any garment intended to fit a 36-in. breast man (over vest) should be marked 36.

(*b*) A boy's suit, overcoat or any garment intended to fit a 30-in. breast boy (over vest), should be marked 30.

2. Trousers, Knickers, etc., belonging to suits.

It is recommended that trousers, knickers, etc., belonging to suits, should be marked with the breast measure of the suit, for example:

(*a*) Trousers for a 36-in. breast man would be marked 36.

(*b*) Knickers for a 30-in. breast boy would be marked 30;

which would facilitate matching up with jacket and vest. The waist measure should also be stated on the ticket, and the leg measure, if thought desirable.

3. Trousers, Knickers, etc., only.

It is recommended that trousers, knickers, etc., other than those belonging or relating to suits, should be marked with waist measure, and if thought desirable, leg measure also.

4. Lettering.

It is recommended that normal or regular size suits or overcoats should bear no mark other than the size, but that:

Long suits or overcoats should be marked “L” after the size.

Short suits or overcoats should be marked “S” after the size.

Thick Set (but normal in height) suits or overcoats should be marked “T” after the size.

The general use of these letters will enable the retailer to become accustomed to them and prevent confusion.

5. Fittings.

While the general adoption of the *breast measure* to identify the size is recommended, no attempt is being made to define regular, long, short, or thick-set sizes other than by *breast measure*, it being recognised that the question of fittings must be left to the manufacturer to deal with according to the requirements of his own particular business.

U.S. DEPARTMENT OF COMMERCE BUREAU OF STANDARDS

Commercial Standard CS 13–30

A joint conference of representative manufacturers, merchants, educators and users adopted a commercial standard for dress patterns. The industry has since accepted, and approved for promulgation by the Department of Commerce, the specifications as shown herein.

The following classifications and corresponding body measurements are recommended as standard for dress patterns:—

LADIES

Bust	34	36	38	40	42	44	46	48	50
Waist	28	30	32	34	36	38	40	42	44
Hip [1]	37	39	41	43	45	47½	50	53	56

MISSES

Size	14	16	18	20
Bust	32	34	36	38
Waist	27	28	30	32
Hip [1]	35	37	39	41
Socket bone to floor [2]	52	54	—	—

JUNIORS

Size	13	15	17
Bust	31	33	35
Waist	26	27½	29
Hip [1]	34	36	38
Socket bone to floor [2]	50	53	—

GIRLS

Size	6	8	10	12	14
Breast	24	26	28	30	32
Waist	24	25	26	26½	27
Socket bone to floor [2]	36	40	44	48	52

CHILDREN

Size	2	3	4	5	6
Breast	21	22	23	23½	24
Waist	21	22	23	23½	24
Socket bone to floor [2]	28	30	32	34	36

INFANTS

Size	½	1	2	3
Breast	19	20	21	22
Waist	19	20	21	22
Socket bone to floor [2]	21	24	28	30

BOYS

Size	6	8	10	12	14	16
Breast	24	26	28	30	32	34
Neck	11	11½	12	12½	13½	14
Waist	24	25	26	27	28	30
Socket bone to floor [2]	36	40	44	48	52	54

LITTLE BOYS

Size	1	2	3	4	5	6
Breast	20	21	22	23	23½	24
Waist	20	21	22	23	23½	24
Socket bone to floor [2]	24	28	30	32	34	36

[1] Hip measurement taken 7 ins. below natural waist line.
[2] Socket bone: uppermost thoracic vertebræ at back of neck. The individual is measured while wearing shoes.

This note is added:

"It is understood that the above recommendation may not coincide with the average of anthropometric measurements from various sources, but is rather a practical compromise between such measurements, the experience of dress pattern manufacturers, and their commercial practice, and will provide approximate dimensions to suit the average requirements bearing in mind that final fit is established by adjustments to suit the individual."

AUTHENTIC FIGURES ISSUED BY THE STYLE RESEARCH BUREAU
UNITED WOMEN'S WEAR LEAGUE OF AMERICA
COMPARISON OF JUNIOR AND MISSES MEASUREMENTS

	JUNIOR				MISS				
Size:	11.	13.	15.	17.	12.	14.	16.	18.	20.
Bust . .	31	32½	34	35½	32½	34	35½	37	38½
Waist . .	25	26½	28	29½	26½	28	29½	31	32½
Hips 9 ins. below waist . .	35	36½	38	39½	35	36½	38	39½	41
Length of waist in back .	14	14	14¼	14¾	15	15¼	15¾	16	16
Across back 5 ins. below neckline .	12	12½	13	13½	12½	13	13½	14	14½

Bust measurements taken as follows:—

Miss forms 8½ ins. below neckline in front.
8 „ „ back.
6¾ „ shoulders.

Junior forms 7½ ins. below neckline front and back.
6 ins. „ shoulders.

3. The table below was compiled in 1919 by the United States Army Medical Department, from data taken from 100,000 demobilised soldiers. The object was to arrive at the dimensions of a number of manikins, each one representing a definite and distinct form-type, with a view to providing military uniforms in suitable sizes. A few exceptional figures, amounting to less than 5 per thousand men measured, were disregarded in compiling the table of sizes.

The dimensions are printed here as the final practical result of the most thorough piece of research in male anthropometry ever attempted. The complete Report, from which this table is taken, may be consulted in the Reference Libraries in our larger cities. A lengthy digest of the Report was made by this writer, and published serially in the trade Press during 1933. This final table, however, was not then published.

Note.—The dimensions were taken in centimetres, and have been converted to inches for the convenience of English students.

MEN'S SUITS

REGULAR

Breast . .	34	35	36	37	38	39	40	41	42	43	44	45	46
Sleeve . .	31	31½	32	32½	32½	33	33½	33½	34	34½	34½	34½	34½
Trs. Waist .	31	32	33	33½	34	36	38	39	41	42	43	44	45
Leg (P.T.U.) .	30	30	30½	31	31	31	31	31	31	30	30	30	30

LONG

Breast . .	34	35	36	37	38	39	40	41	42	43	44	45	46
Sleeve . .	32	32½	33	33½	33½	34	34½	34½	35	35½	35½	35½	35½
Trs. Waist	31	31½	32½	33	34	35	36	37	38½	39½	41	42	43
Leg (P.T.U.) .	31½	31½	32	32½	32½	32½	32½	32½	32½	31½	31½	31½	31½

SHORT

Breast	34	35	36	37	38	39	40	41	42	43	44	45	46
Sleeve	30	30½	31	31½	31½	32	32½	32½	33	33½	33½	33½	33½
Trs. Waist	32	33	34	34½	35	37	39	40	41	42	43	44	45
Leg (P.T.U.)	28½	28½	29	29½	29½	29½	29½	29½	29½	28½	28½	28½	28½

STOUT

Breast	36	37	38	39	40	41	42	43	44	45	46
Sleeve	32	32½	32½	33	33½	33½	34	34½	34½	34½	34½
Trs. Waist	35	36	38	39	40	41	42	43	44	45	46
Leg (P.T.U.)	30½	31	31	31	31	31	31	30	30	30	30

SHORT STOUT

Breast	36	37	38	39	40	41	42	43	44	45	46
Sleeve	31	31½	31½	32	32½	32½	33	33½	33½	33½	33½
Trs. Waist	36	37	38	39	40	41	42	43	44	45	46
Leg (P.T.U.)	29	29½	29½	29½	29½	29½	29½	28½	28½	28½	28½

BOYS AND YOUTHS

Size	4	5	6	7	8	9	10	11	12	13	14
Breast	26	27	28	29	30	31	32	32½	33	34	35
Sleeve	23½	25½	26	27	28	29	30	30½	31	31½	32
Trs. Waist	26½	26½	27	27½	28	28½	29½	30	30½	31	31½
Leg (P.T.U.)	25	26	26	27½	28	28½	29	29½	30	31	31½

The leg lengths in the above chart sizes should be related to the formula given for Cuffed Hem (P.T.U.) on pp. 122–3.

5. One of the best-known British mantle firms issues a scale of sizes from which the following are taken:

MAIDS' SIZES

Size:	5.	6.	7.	8.	9.
Breast	29	30	31	32	33
Bust	30	31	32	33	34
Waist	26	26	26	27	28
Hips	36	37	38	39	40
In Sleeve	15	16	16½	17	17
Nape to Waist	13¾	13	14	14½	15

WOMEN'S SIZES

Fitting:	SS	SSX	SM	SW	SWX	W	WM	WFB	WX	SOS	OS	XOS	OSM	XXOS	XOSM	XXXOS
Breast	32	32	33	34	34	35½	33	38	36	38	38	41	42	43	45	45
Bust	34	34	35	36	36	38	35	42	38	41	41	44	45	47	50	50
Waist	29	29	30	30	30	32	30	32	32	34	35	36	36	38	39	40
Hips	40	42	44	42	44	44	44	46	47	47	47	50	52	53	56	60
In sleeve	17	17	16½	17½	17½	17½	16½	17½	17½	15½	17	17½	17	17½	17	17

Reference:

SS	= Slim small.
SSX	= ditto, with larger hips.
SM	= Small matron.
SW	= Slim woman.
SWX	= ditto, with larger hips.
W	= Woman, standard size.
WM	= Woman of matronly figure.
WFB	= Woman, full bust.
WX	= W size, with larger hips.
SOS	= Short outsize.
OS	= Outsize.
XOS	= Extra outsize.
OSM	= Outsize matronly figure.

SIZE AND MOVEMENT

Movement

THE necessity for considering the movements of the joints will be evident when it is realised that the clothing of these moving parts must be so arranged as to permit free movement of the body. (Figs. 3, 4 and 5.)

The normal movements of the arms, for example, are upwards and forwards. In the construction of both the sleeve and scye a skin fit cannot be aimed at, because it would restrain arm movement. A little drapery is, therefore, arranged at the back of the outer sleeve and a small amount is left on the under sleeve. These amounts are utilised when the arm is moved forwards or upwards, yet are not so great as to be unsightly when the arm is at rest.

No such arrangement is needed at the front of scye, there being no normal backward movement of the arm to warrant it.

The raising of the knee to a position that will bring the thigh parallel to the ground will furnish a further example. This movement causes an extension of the seat muscles, and consequently the necessity for greater length in the seat of the garment. The amount that, in the body's normal position, takes the form of lateral drapery is brought into use as soon as the expansion of the seat muscles takes place. This is part of the provision made by using an appropriate seat angle.

In the knee of a pair of riding-breeches or pantaloons provision must be made for the bending of the joint. The only possible movement of the knee results in lengthening over the front of the joint and shortening behind. In any leg garment, therefore, that is secured to the body at the waist (above) and at the hollow (below) there must be an amount added to the front of the garment to permit of this lengthening. It is usual, too, in view of the corresponding shortening in the rear, for an amount, in the form of a lateral dart, to be removed from behind the knee.

To extend the illustration: The position of the body in the saddle must be taken into account in the construction of equestrian leg garments. All sorts of joint movements then take place, some of them abnormal, but they must all be reflected in the finished garment.

Where the limbs are not closely fitted, but are clothed in drapery, as the trousers leg or coat sleeve, no special provision is necessary, as the drapery readily permits of free movement.

Both the usual and the exceptional movements of the joints should be studied with a view to the production of satisfactory garments that will permit of free movement and yet not appear excessively large. Provision for the special balance requirements of altered attitude, or open-ness of leg construction in leg garments, are two further illustrations of allowances for movement of the joints.

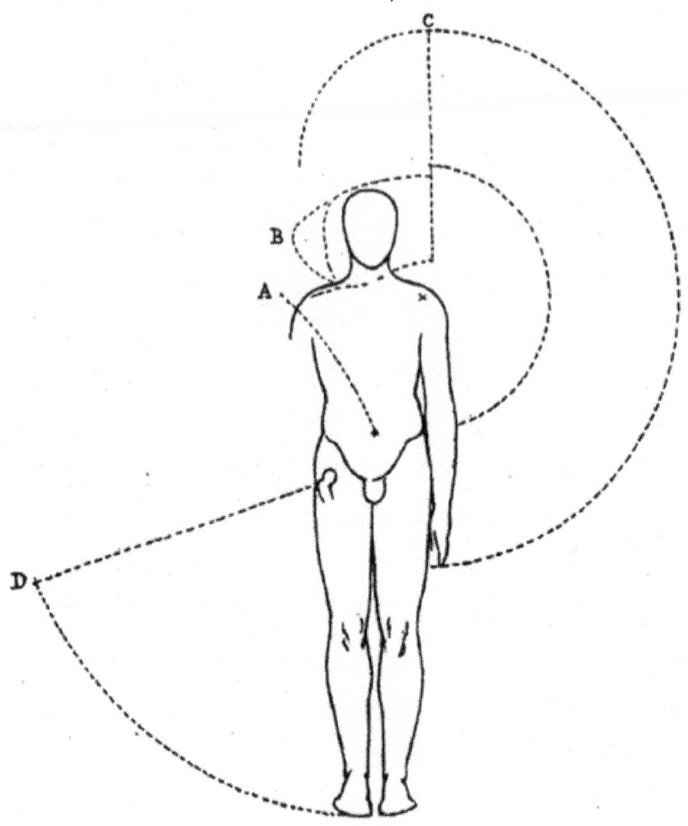

FIG. 3.

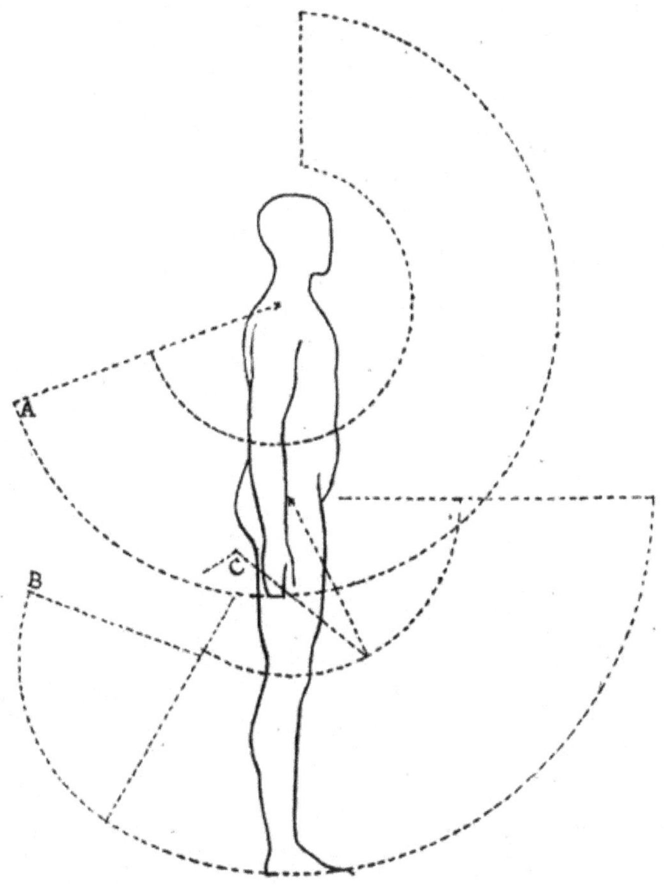

FIG. 4.

Tolerances

A tolerance is the agreed amount by which the girth of a garment shall exceed the actual girth measurements of the body. A measurement is taken over a waistcoat, for example; a lounge jacket to be worn over this garment will need to be a greater girth than the exact measurement.

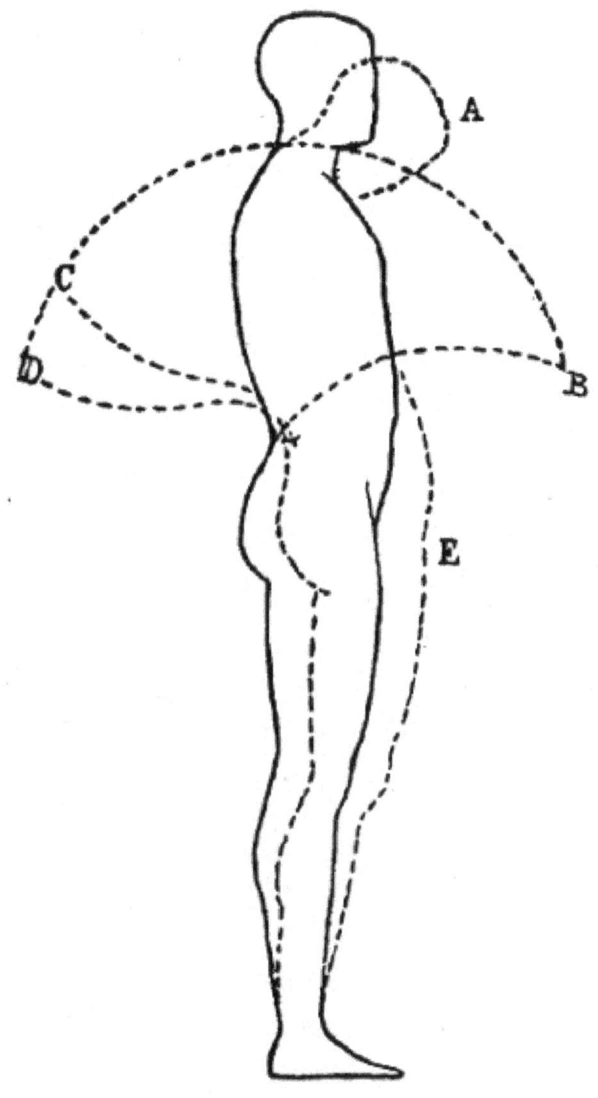

FIG. 5.

A garment which is worn over another garment should be larger than the garment over which it fits. This difference is called a tolerance.

An illustration from mechanical engineering may help. The circumference of a cylinder must exceed slightly that of the piston; otherwise fitting would be impossible. Even though the materials of which cylinders and clothes are made are not similar, yet the same principle operates. A diagram showing a section of the body and the garment will make this clear.

The amount here dealt with is for fitting: An amount of about 2 ins. on the girth measures, or 1 in. on the half garment, will usually be sufficient, and all garment systems provide for at least this amount.

A fitting tolerance is distributed generally over the garment; it is not deposited locally. The normal working out of a system will ensure its automatic and even distribution throughout the girth of a garment.

This tolerance for fitting should not be confused with allowances for seams or extra easiness of fitting.

The trousers waist is, perhaps, the only body girth where an exception is made and no tolerance left. This is because a close trousers waist is generally desired, and also, that another garment has to fit over the waist.

Height and Contour Length

The division of the total height of the body into equal sections will have impressed the ideas of the unity of the body and the harmony and proportion of its parts and sections. It should be pointed out, however, that the height of any section is not the same as the contour length of the same section.

Examples may be taken from many parts of the body. Fig. 6 shows the difference between the height and the contour length of the nape to breast section.

AB = height = 8 1/2 ins.

AC = 8 1/2 ins. + 5/8 in. = 9 1/8 ins.

AC = 8 1/2 ins. + 5/8 in. + 3/8 in. = 9 1/2 ins.

The garment designer has to provide for the contour lengths of the body, and the measures he takes on the surface of the body are actually contour lengths. When, therefore, he is making provision in respect of height, it will be necessary to make certain additions. The nearer the contour of the body approaches to the vertical, the less will require to be added: the more curved the contour, the greater will be the addition. For example, the round back of a stooping figure will require more garment length in that section; the straight back of the over-erect figure will require less.

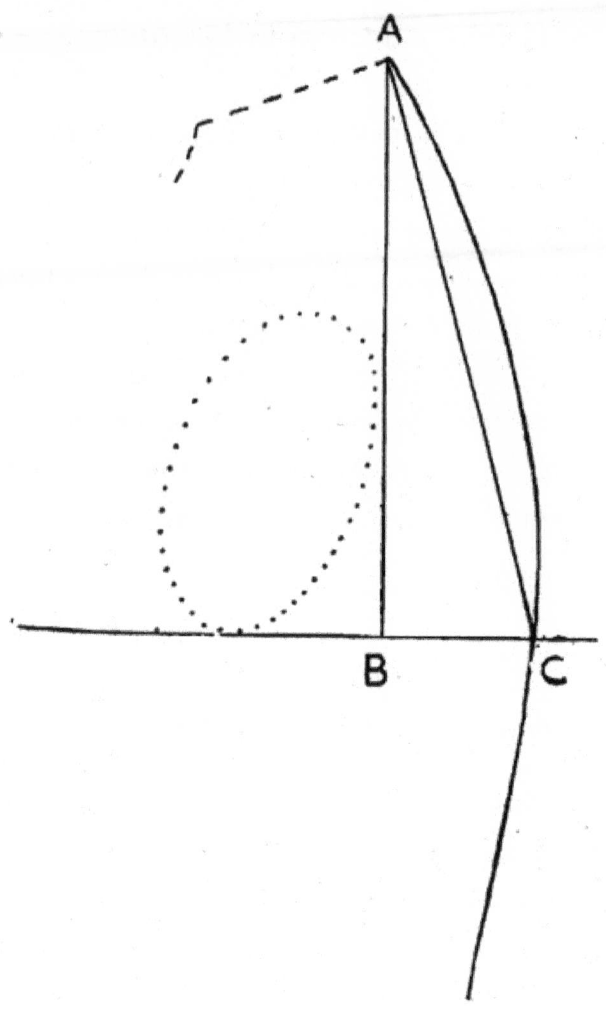

FIG. 6.

The Relation of the Garment to the Body

Fitting and Draping.

A garment may be closely or loosely related to the body: it may be a fitting garment, or a draped garment; or it may be described as semi-fitting, which covers a variety of intermediate effects between fitting and draping.

A garment, or part of a garment, may be said to *fit* the body when the garment, or the part, follows closely the contours of the body.

A garment may be said to be *draped* when material in excess of the body's minimum requirements is introduced. For example:—

A vest may be called a fitting garment, as it must follow closely the contours of the body. No drapery may be permitted in a vest.

A lounge jacket will fit the body in that part which lies between the neck and the breast; below that part it may be fitting, or it may contain some little excess drapery.

A pair of trousers will fit the body closely in the waist. Between waist and seat prominence there will be a small amount of excess girth, while below the seat the legs are draped to a degree decided by the fashion of the moment.

Few garments may strictly be termed fitting; and perhaps no single garment may be described as completely draped. Even the circular cape fits the neck and the shoulders, below which it drapes. The Scots "plaid", really a shawl, certainly drapes entirely—but is it a garment?

Control.

A garment is controlled by that section in which it most nearly fits the body.

The "hang" of a pair of trousers is controlled by the waist to seat section. Any wrong construction, deficiency in length or girth, excess in girth or length in this section, will disturb the correct draping of the legs.

The lounge jacket is controlled by the neck to breast section. Below this line the garment line may diverge from the body contour and become a more or less draped garment. Any misconstruction in the control region would become apparent by effects observed in the draped part. It is obvious, then, that in the construction of the control section of a garment the closest attention should be paid to securing the correct lengths and girths, seeing that the success of the garment as a whole depends on its correct construction.

THE GARMENT PATTERN

A garment pattern is a full-size replica, in paper or cardboard, of the garment for which it is cut. There will normally be a pattern for every part of the garment.

Seams (or turnings) and *inlays* and *upturns may* be included in the pattern.

When the parts of a garment are sewn together, an amount, varying from 1/4 in. to 1/2 in., according to the type of garment and the material, is required over the sewing mark. This amount is called a seam or turning. Most pattern systems provide for an allowance for seams in the working out of the system: others, mainly systems for women's garments, produce a nett pattern to which seams must be added. Various kinds of outside finish of seams include pressed open, overlaid, stitched or slated: the material used and the effect desired will suggest the type of seam used.

An inlay is an amount of material left on over and above the requirements of a seam, to provide for any enlargement or reduction of the garment.

An upturn is an amount left on at the hem of a garment, or sleeve, to face the hem and to permit of lengthening, if necessary.

A pattern lay is an arrangement, on the material, of a set of pattern parts, laid-in with a view to economy of material.

Different widths, designs, and textures of fabrics; various sizes in single garments and in mixed quantities; differing types of garment, all enter into the successful arrangement of a pattern lay.

A pattern will contain two quite different sets of factors, and should therefore be regarded from two distinct points of view, namely:—

(1) the anatomical basis of the pattern, and
(2) the style features embodied in the pattern.

(1) Anatomical Basis.

The first consideration is that the pattern shall be made with the physical requirements of the body in mind. Certain parts and points of all garments must be located with regard to the anatomical requirements of the figure. The demands of size must first be met, and the various parts of the pattern located with reference to the corresponding parts of the body. For example, in a trunk garment the size and shape of the shoulder must be reproduced in the garment, the armhole (scye) correctly placed, and the size of the neck provided for. These parts of the garment are clearly related to the parts of the body concerned, and must be so regarded. The measurements taken on the body, together with certain derived or inferred measures, reproduced in the appropriate places on the pattern, will secure that the main anatomical features of the body have been provided for.

Construction Lines.

Construction lines should be regarded as the girder work of pattern construction: they are the framework within which the basis of the pattern is drawn. The construction lines reproduce, on the pattern, the lines on which the measurements were taken on the body. Construction lines should be kept to a minimum: no more than are necessary to lay a proper basis should be used.

(2) The Style Features of the Pattern.

When the various anatomical points have been located on the construction lines, a basis has been laid down on which the desired style features may be superimposed. It must be recognised that in pattern-making there is much that is drawing, pure and simple. The arrangement of style features should be regarded as drawing, and not as related to the anatomical basis of the pattern. A constructional system, properly understood, does not concern itself with features that will change with current fashion: its function is to provide a sound basis to which any fashion feature may be added.

Style features may be regarded as those parts of a garment which possess, primarily, a decorative value, but which are not strictly related to the anatomy of the figure.

The shape of a coat front, the fall of the collar, the size and shape of the lapel, the arrangement and type of pockets, the finish of a cuff, the run of neck in a vest are examples of style features.

Most systems of pattern-making, in addition to providing an anatomical basis for the pattern, make some provision for securing and locating style features. The natural result of this traditional approach has been that the two elements have hardly been regarded as distinct, each from the other. The student should regard each separately and form an estimate of the relative value of each. Rather different mental qualities are called for in each direction: construction is based on geometry, while style has affinities with art.

It will have been observed that two garments may have an identical anatomical basis and yet have entirely different style features. The student will do well, therefore, to cultivate the faculty of observation in this matter, so that he may learn to distinguish between the two different aspects of his work of pattern-making.

A base pattern is one in which only the basic anatomical features of the body are reflected and provided for.

A garment pattern is a base pattern with the desired style features added.

Points to Observe in Pattern-Making

The ability to put down correctly placed construction lines and to fix all points accurately on those lines is to the credit of the young student. But as will soon be apparent this aspect of pattern-making is but a well-laid foundation. A garment is a success mainly in whether it achieves a good sense of line. The fact is that pattern-making is mainly good free-hand drawing with the crayon. The constructional points must not only be correctly placed, but they must be connected with free, graceful lines. Artistry of a high order is demanded in the drawing of every seam line, every front, lapel, collar. It is not sufficient merely to connect points with any sort of line; it must be done tastefully. It is the business of the artist to secure effects and his means are counted secondary to the end aimed at.

Whenever a line is being drawn it is a good plan to *keep in mind the silhouette line of the body* that is being followed on the pattern, and to try to get the body line on to paper. The next idea, *of modifying* a body line to secure any particular style effect, will follow naturally. To these ends the young student will make a special study of the curved contours of the body and seek to reproduce them in line. The most capable of pattern-makers will always spend a little time "sweetening his lines", as the old trade phrase runs. This sense of line can be trained only by continual practice.

This applies not only to long seams, edges, etc., but also to seam-runs connecting adjacent parts. The curves should be made continuous as though no seam existed.

Checking Seam Lengths.

Care should be taken to balance the two sides of a seam for length. Part should be laid on part with balance notches fairly placed, all seam lengths checked and all parts harmonised.

Notches.

(*a*) Notches are placed in various parts of garments, so that the machinist may sew the various parts together in their correct relationship.

(*b*) Where one part is longer than its related part (*e.g.*, shoulder seam, sleeve head), notches are placed to localise correctly the excess length of the one part.

In (*a*) the notches are placed to ensure that a correct *balance* is maintained during manufacture.

In (*b*) the notches are used to ensure that the desired *shape* is secured in manufacture.

Position of Notches.

The lateral construction lines of the pattern usually localise the balance notches.

Trousers: Fork, knee, hem.

Breeches: Fork, knee, hollow, calf, hem.

Vest: Breast, waist.

Coats: Breast, waist, hip, elbow.

Sleeve: Where the forearm seam is displaced from its normal position, notches should be made in the top- and under-sleeve about 5 ins. from top of seam and from cuff.

Shoulder seam: Length of back will exceed length of front by varying amounts, dependent on type of figure. This excess, whatever it is, should be localised by notches placed 1 in. from shoulder end and 1 1/2 ins. from neck end of seam.

Sleeve: Notches should be placed in back and forepart scyes to show positions of forearm and hindarm seams of sleeve. A notch in top sleeve should harmonise with shoulder seam of coat. Notches should be placed in forepart and top sleeve about 2 ins. above front pitch.

Note.—Time taken in carefully going over, and checking, all the details of a pattern is well spent, from every point of view.

The Centre Line in Construction.

The important points in a pattern should, wherever possible, be grouped round, and related to, a central construction line which corresponds with a definite body line. This grouping round a given centre would appear to be the most natural way of approaching any constructional task; in the drawing of a garment pattern it is really the only practical method of procedure.

In a trunk garment, the centre-back construction line follows the line of the spine: all back construction is based on this line. The centre-front line, which corresponds, in the pattern, to a line on the body from the fonticulus to the navel, is the basis and starting-point for all types of front construction.

In leg garment construction, the front and side seams can be more accurately placed when their positions are fixed with reference to a middle front line. A centre leg construction line gives better opportunity for a correct distribution of leg width drapery around a given centre than either a side or front construction line.

Front Construction I

The variety of cases of disproportion between breast and waist girths is very wide. If, say, a 38-in. breast girth is taken as a standard, it will be quite possible to find a dozen different form-types, all of the same breast girth, but each with a different waist girth. They will range from the young athlete of ideal proportion who measures 32 ins. or less at the waist, to the sedentary man in middle life whose waist girth is equal to his breast girth.

Beyond that, again, is the range of corpulent figures, where the waist girth will exceed the breast by varying amounts. To merely say that in a certain case the waist is disproportionate to the breast girth is to say little: the *amount* of the disproportion is the important matter.

Take, for example, the figure of a man 5 ft. 8 ins. high, 38 ins. breast, 34 ins. waist. He would be regarded as a "regular" size or a proportionate figure.

Now assume that the height and breast measurements remain stationary but that the waist girth increases by say 2 ins. This 2 ins. must be included in the dimensions of the garment, at the waist. The traditional formula for the addition of excess waist over the proportionate is that two-thirds are required at the front and one-third at the side. Experience would appear to confirm this in the great majority of cases.

Were a greater number of seams available for the purpose, it may be possible to distribute the excess a little more widely and exactly, but for all practical purposes we are restricted to the front and side only.

If none but ideal figures claimed our attention the same method of front construction would apply in all cases. But it will be obvious that a different amount will be needed on the front waist of a 38 breast, 37 waist, than where the dimensions are 38 breast and 32 waist. There is in this case a difference of 5 ins. waist girth on a similar breast measurement—*i.e.*, 2 1/2 ins. on the half coat. This amount, then, must be distributed between front and side in correct ratio.

The principle may be crystallised as follows: disproportion is present as soon as the proportionate ratio between two related measurements is disturbed. If 38 breast, 34 waist, is a proportionate relationship, then 38 breast, 36 waist must indicate that the waist is disproportionately large by 2 ins. This disproportion must be reflected in the pattern at the appropriate places: the amount allotted to the side is automatically placed by directly measuring up on the waist line of the pattern.

The provision made for corpulency is an extension of the same idea, but to an abnormal degree. The main principle involved is that disproportion begins immediately proportion is disturbed, and that adequate provision for this disproportion must be made at the appropriate places.

In "long" sizes the ratio of waist girth to breast girth will be a little less than in the "regular" figure; in "short" sizes, a little more.

Front Construction II

The widths of a garment at the breast and waist from centre back construction line to centre front will be the total of

(*a*) half the girth of the body,

(*b*) an allowance for seams,

(*c*) an appropriate tolerance for fitting.

This centre front line will be taken as the base for all front construction. The centre-front garment will coincide, on the drawn pattern, with a line on the body drawn from the fonticulus to the navel. If this line were regarded as the front edge of the garment, the edges would meet, but would not over-wrap. In front of this line, then, the front of the garment will be constructed.

The normal fastening is by means of a button and a buttonhole: this necessitates that the fronts shall over-wrap.

The neck (or shank) of the button fits directly into the eye of the buttonhole. In most garments there will be some difference between the distance of the eye of the buttonhole from the edge of the garment and the distance of the button from the front edge.

Both fronts are, however, cut to the same size, the only exception being the vest, where an *extra* button stand is frequently allowed on the right side.

If the requirements of the button were left on one side and the needs of the buttonhole on the other, two fronts of unequal size would result. The lapels, too, would be unequal in size and different in shape. The two fronts of a garment are, therefore, cut equal: the total of the fastening allowances (*i.e.*, the B.S. and B.H.S.) being divided equally between the two fronts.

A garment of which the fronts are cut equal in size and the amounts of B.S. and B.H.S. are equal, will fasten centrally—*i.e.*, a vertical line drawn through the centres of the buttons will coincide with the centre front line of the body.

A garment of which the fronts are cut equal in size, but has a B.S. greater than B.H.S., cannot fasten centrally.

Definitions.

Button Stand. The distance from the centre of the button to the garment edge.

Buttonhole Stand. The distance from the eye of the buttonhole to the garment edge.

Buttons Apart (in D.B. garments). The distance between the centres of opposite buttons.

Wrap. The amount by which the fronts overlay when the garment is fastened, measured from edge to edge.

The distance from the eye of the buttonhole to the edge will, of course, vary in different garments. The following amounts should be regarded as minima:—

vest, 1/2 in.

lounge, 3/4 in.

over-garment 1 in.

The buttonhole stand will always be half width of button plus *at least* 1/4 in.

(A soft roll lapel will, of course, demand more than the quarter inch.)

The length of the buttonhole will depend on the size and type of button used.

The sizes of buttons generally used are:—

vest, 22 lines.

lounge, 30 lines,

over-garments, 45–70 lines,

breeches (knee) 16–18 lines.

The button used should, as to size and shape, harmonise with the character of the garment.

Button sizes may be simply estimated by taking the 40 lines size as a standard, thus:—

30 lines, 3/4 ins. diameter (the size of a sixpenny piece)

40 lines, 1 in. ins. diameter (the size of a halfpenny piece)

50 lines, 1 1/4 ins. diameter (the size of a half-crown piece)

60 lines, 1 1/2 ins. diameter

Larger and smaller sizes in the same ratio.

When a fancy button, of dome, acorn, or ball shape, is used, a longer buttonhole is needed than when a relatively flat button is used.

Formulæ for Front Construction.

Assume a centre front garment line already placed.

(1) For S.B.1 Front:—

$$\frac{\text{B.S.}^{1}\text{ plus B.H.S.}^{1}\text{ plus 2 seams}}{2} = \text{amount allowed beyond centre line.}$$

(2) For D.B.1 Front:—
½ buttons apart plus B.H.S. plus 1 seam = amount allowed beyond centre line.

Examples:—

(*a*) S.B. Vest, buttons 3/4 in. on from edge.

Button stand	**¾ in.**
Buttonhole	**½ in.**
2 seams	**½ in.**
= total for 2 fronts	**1¾ ins.**

$$\frac{1\frac{3}{4}\text{ ins.}}{2} = \frac{7}{8}\text{ in. total allowance beyond centre line.}$$

1 S.B. = Single breasted; D.B. = Double breasted; B.S. = Button stand. See definitions above; B.H.S. = Buttonhole stand.

(*b*) S.B. Lounge Jacket, buttons 1 1/2 ins. on from edge.

Button stand	**1½ ins.**
Buttonhole	**¾ in.**
2 seams	**½ in.**
= total for 2 fronts	**2¾ ins.**

$$\frac{2\frac{3}{4}\text{ ins.}}{2} = 1\frac{3}{8}\text{ ins. total allowance beyond centre line.}$$

(*c*) D.B. Lounge Jacket, buttons 6 ins. apart.

½ buttons apart 3 ins.
Buttonhole stand ¾ in.
1 seam ¼ in.

4 ins. = total allowance beyond centre line.

(*d*) S.B. Over-garment, buttons 4 1/2 ins. on.

Button stand 4½ ins.
Buttonhole stand 1 in.
2 seams ½ in.

= total for 2 fronts 6 ins / 2 = 3 ins.: total allowance beyond centre line.

(3) Linked Front.

This type carries a buttonhole in each front. The fastening is effected by means of two buttons linked together by a "neck". This neck should be twice the length of the buttonhole stand. When the buttons are passed through the buttonholes, the fronts are fastened and the edges will meet exactly.

If it is desired, for style purposes, to secure a slight tightening of the garment when fastened, the connecting neck of the buttons may be shortened. If this tightening of the garment is *not* desired, yet a short neck required between the buttons, an additional 1/4 in. or 3/8 in. may be added to each front.

Lapel Construction.

The lapel is a style feature, and in the construction of a pattern should be so regarded. It is in no way related to the anatomical groundwork of the pattern. In a garment that has no lapel, of the close-throat or lancer-front types, for example, the centre front line upwards from the breast to the fonticulus and the gorge from the neck point round the base of the neck column to the fonticulus are of great importance; and the success of the pattern depends on those lines being correctly placed with reference to the anatomy of the thorax. In the case of a lapel, however, the garment, for all constructional purposes, does not extend in front of the crease row. The placing of the seam which joins the lapel to the collar is purely a matter of taste, and is regulated by current fashion.

The following order of procedure should be followed when constructing the lapel on a pattern:—

(1) Place the crease row in its correct position having regard to

(*a*) the collar stand and (*b*) the length of the lapel;

(2) draw an appropriate lapel in its first position on the forepart;

(3) transfer the lapel to its second position on the opposite

side of the crease row;

(4) arrange for any dart necessary for the creation of shape by suppressing the gorge. It is seldom necessary to remove more than 1/24 of half breast measurement in a dart.

GARMENT BALANCE

THORNTON, in his *International System*, defines the various aspects of garment balance with regard to definite types of figure. Size, shape, and attitude are taken into account in their usual and unusual forms.

As a general definition, he gives: garment balance is "the adjustment, in harmony with the natural attitude of the figure, of the back and front lengths".

Proportionate Balance.

"This has relation to the size of any draft pattern, or figure. It is correct, or incorrect, as the case may be, when judged by a given proportion of the breast circumference of such draft, etc. But it takes no cognisance of specific forms, which, although identical as to size, may vary less or more in their figuration. It is proportionate as determined by any given system."

Normal Balance.

"This is really equipoise. When the front and back depth sections which control balance equal each other, then we have normal balance; although these depth quantities may not be proportionate to the breast circumference. For example: suppose a model of 21 ins. breast has its scye depths reckoned from the base or breast line at 10 ins. Here this 10 ins. is disproportionate but normal."

Particular Balance.

"Has relation to the specific form about to be fitted. It is evident that we could have a figure, pattern, or draft that could be unequal in its balance quantities. It would not be either strictly proportionate nor normal. Or, we could have another one that would be normal, but not proportionate to its general size. A particular balance is correct when it is rightly adjusted to the special figure dealt with.

"Again, in defining balance there is still much vagueness as to the points or lines where the back and front quantities should be reckoned from. The two first-quoted definitions are inadequate, because they only recognise the completed garment: they are general, not exact. The third one is nearer the mark, as it takes notice of component parts which are, of course, the factors in all form variations. For example: Take a proportionate coat model 36 ins. breast with base, or scye line, marked upon it. Experts agree pretty well that, dating from this base line upward, the vertical length of the front of coat or pattern should be 1/4 in. more than the corresponding back section. This is so in the sectional system, where the back boundary line of the scye, is seen as 1/4 in. shorter than the line which governs the front of scye, and both of these lengths have a set proportion to the scye or breast measure. This, therefore, illustrates a *normal balance.*

"But suppose we have to do with a short figure, here the two governing lines of the scye depth will be less than that set proportion; but they may still bear the same proportion to each other. This will be an illustration of a *short normal balance.*

"Or, we may have a long figure, where the vertical lines are longer in respect to the normal, also to the actual size, yet still to each other similarly proportioned. This will be *a long normal figure.*

"Then we may get to particular balances. The back short, and the front long, and the two lengths varying in different forms; or the reverse, front short and back long. And in attaining the ultimate object, which is the equipoise of the finished garment, these little items and distinctions have to be kept in mind.

"*Proportionate balance*, has relation to size, *particular* balance has relation to specific forms, or the natural figures of our clients."1

The principles of balance, then, operate in the control section of a garment.

This section controls the draped part of the garment dependent from it. It follows, therefore, that the relative lengths of back and front of the garment in the control section shall accord with the contour requirements of the figure; otherwise the drapery which is controlled from the section above will not be evenly distributed around the body. It is necessary, then, in order to secure a garment which hangs correctly on the figure, to ensure that the back and front lengths of the garment shall harmonise with the back and front contour lengths of the figure.

These lengths, in the *proportionate figure*, bear a certain relationship to each other. This assumes that the proportionate figure normally stands in a certain way—*i.e.*, an erect posture. Most constructional systems automatically provide for this correct balance of the proportionate figure. If this posture be altered in either a forward or backward direction, it follows that the previous proportionate equipoise between the two lengths has been disturbed. The amounts then may have to be lengthened or shortened to harmonise with the altered attitude of the figure. Balance, therefore, may be affected by an altered posture.

Increased or decreased contour lengths—due, *e.g.*, on the one hand to abnormal abdominal development, or, on the other, to a stooping attitude—will require that the front length of the garment in the control section shall be longer or shorter than the back length by the amount needed to compensate for these variations from the normal.

A local abnormality (*e.g.*, round back) or a physical deformity (*e.g.*, hump back) will demand a longer back control length, than would be required by the normal proportionate figure.

It will be obvious, therefore, that the balance requirements of figures vary with the contour and the attitude of the form. A comparison of the balance requirements of the boy and man will emphasise the effect of the growth, and particularly the development of the figure upon its balance requirements.

Where a proportion of a scale based upon a breast girth is taken for adjusting the relation between the front and back balance lengths, it will be found imperfect, in so far as it takes no account of attitude beyond that of the proportionate figure. A scale, derived on the assumption that the body is proportionate in its dimensions, also assumes the proportionate attitude. Any departure from this proportionate attitude must be provided for outside of and apart from the working-scale quantities.

Compensation for Change of Attitude.

A change of attitude, involving a lengthening of one control length, and therefore a corresponding shortening of the other control length to maintain equipoise, suggests a recognition of *compensation*. There does not appear to be sufficient reason to support the idea that the compensation shall be equal—*i.e.*, that what the back gains from a forward change of attitude, the front loses.

Take, for example, the most common of variations from the normally erect stance, the slight forward stoop in the breast and shoulder sections. The back contour will lengthen and the front contour will shorten. The lengthening of the back contour is, however, limited by the bone and cartilage structure of the spinal column. The vertebræ of the spine are, as it were, hinged to each other: they may, however, be extended only to the limits of their cartilagenous connections. The front contour, on the other hand, shortens and becomes more nearly vertical. The rib-structure sinks into the unresisting mass of the abdomen. This could be argued at considerable length, but sufficient grounds have been given to enable the student to follow up the matter for himself.

On the other hand, a change of attitude may take the form of over-erectness. Here again it may reasonably be assumed that the front contour is capable of lengthening to a greater degree than the back shortens. The very structure of the spine presupposes a limit to the shortening of the back contour; while the front of the body is not supported in the same way and to the same extent.

It may be assumed, therefore, that in any departure from the normally erect stance of the proportionate figure, whether forward or backward, the front will be affected to a greater degree than the back. This must be recognised in any suggested allowances in respect of deviation from normal erectness. Ruling out deformity and excessive abnormality, and having only in mind the changes in attitude which are often found in the regular, long, short, and stout groups, it is suggested that *length changes in the front contour are twice the amount of any length changes in the back.* That is to say, if, for slight forward stoop, an addition of 1/4 in. is made to the back length, 1/2 in. will be subtracted from the front.

If, for over-erectness, 1/4 in. is deducted from the back control length, 1/2 in. will be added to the front.

Balance Operating in the Hip Section.

Departure from the normal provision made for the proportionate figure may have to be made when there is any departure from the normal erect posture *from the hip joints.* This variation, however, is comparatively rare. In the case of this very unusual figure the forward bending is from the hip joint, which is situated nearly centrally in the body between front and back. The amounts by which the front will be shortened and the back lengthened will be approximately equal.

The extra back length is secured by arranging a larger seat angle; the front is shortened by taking out a wedge on the fork line, the centre front line being tilted forward.

Effects of Incorrect Balance.

(*a*) Assume a jacket designed for a regular figure of normal posture placed on a man whose head was forward and whose back was round, the following symptoms may be expected: If garment were buttoned: the collar would stand away from the nape of neck and would be too low; the crease row of collar and lapel would appear to be too long. If garment were not buttoned: the jacket would stand away from the seat, and the front edges, instead of being parallel, would gradually diverge from the top button to the front hem.

A slight excess of material may also be present at the top of the front sleeve seam.

(*b*) If the same jacket were placed on an over-erect figure, the effects would be exactly opposite. In addition, excess length of back would show in the form of lateral corrugations in the back waist.

1 Thornton, *International System*, p. 361.

MEASUREMENT

THE measurements necessary for the construction of a garment pattern must be collected with the greatest care: only with accurate data can a successful pattern be made.

Accuracy.

The maker of clothing uses plastic material to clothe a plastic body. The engineer, for example, on the other hand is restricted to the use of rigid materials. This difference between the materials used will indicate the degree of accuracy required in each case. The engineer will frequently be required to approach accuracy as nearly as one-thousandth of an inch. The maker of clothing will not, having regard to his materials and his task, feel it necessary to make so near an approach. It will, however, be regarded as of the first importance to take all measurements of the body or of the garment as accurately as possible.

A set of measurements should in a real sense be a description of the body. A body may be described in words (*i.e.*, verbally), by an illustration (*i.e.*, graphically), or by measurements (*i.e.*, mathematically). Measurement should give accurate dimensions from which a pattern may be constructed. Its importance should not be under-estimated;

every dimension taken should be capable of being used either directly in construction, or indirectly for comparative purposes. The dimensions should therefore be taken *fairly—i.e.*, the tape should not be held too closely to the body, nor should it be permitted to be slack. In some girth measurements particularly, the tape should be checked in its position and not permitted to drop below its correct line at the back.

No allowances in any particular direction should be made when taking measures. These must be taken fairly and should, as far as figures can, describe the body. Any alteration to the dimensions in respect of close or easy fitting should be made from correctly taken measurements. Measurements are frequently kept for future reference and use; if any particular allowance had been made while measuring, any future reference to the measurements would result in inaccuracy, because the measures did not fairly represent the figure.

Direct Measurements.

Direct measurements are those data taken from the body or the garment and used directly on the pattern. The relation between the position of the construction lines on the pattern and the placing of the tape on the body when measuring, should be clearly appreciated, because the great majority of measurements are applied on construction lines.

Derived Dimensions.

There are, however, certain parts of the pattern in respect of which no direct measurements have been taken. For example, no measurement may be taken to assist in placing the scye either as to size or its position in the garment. No measurement need necessarily be taken of the girth of the neck or of the width of the back, although the latter may be useful for style purposes. These parts could have been measured, but the difficulty of taking accurate measurements and the greater difficulty of applying them even if taken correctly, renders the use of direct measures for locating certain parts of the garment unreliable.

Such data are called derived measurements. In the case of the normally developed body it is possible to construct the gorge, scye and shoulder of a pattern by means of derived measures. It is recognised that in the proportionate body these parts are in a known relationship to the breast girth measurement. Using this knowledge it is possible to utilise these measurements which are derived from the breast girth dimension for locating those parts which are assumed to be proportionate to the breast girth, and for which no direct measures have been taken.

The Body and the Garment.

It would be well to think of measurements as either body measurements or garment measures. For example, the measurement from the nape to the waist length would be a body measurement—*i.e.*, the distance between two definite positions on the body. The length of a jacket or overcoat, on the other hand, will vary with the fashion of the moment and may be regarded as a garment measure.

The style of a garment will decide what measurements are necessary. For example, garments fastening to the throat demand that a neck (or collar) girth measurement shall be taken; and the position of the fonticulus is sufficiently important to require a direct measurement. The length of the front points of a dress coat, too, can be measured as easily as can the front points on a waistcoat. Again, leg garments, closely fitting the knee, hollow, or calf, will need special measurements.

Special measurements should be taken in respect of physical abnormalities. The position of a *hump* back (whether central or to one side) can be located by a vertical measurement from the nape and laterally from the spine. The prominence of a *hunch* back is best fixed by a measurement from the nape. A measurement from the nape down the spine to the scye depth level could well be made in these cases.

Check Measurements.

A check measurement is taken for purposes of comparison with other measurements. Such comparison may reveal disproportion, and the amount by which the body being measured varies from the proportionate form. For example, if a man of 36 ins. breast girth is wearing a size 17 ins. collar, and it is obviously not too large, then a comparison of the two girths points to abnormal neck development. Again, the 36 ins. breast girth would connote a proportionate middle shoulder measurement of 27 ins.; if it was found that his actual shoulder measure was 29 1/2 ins., the fact of disproportion would be evident, and also the amount by which the actual shoulder exceeded proportion. The scye circumference is another instance of the type of measurement that may be used for checking purposes. The check measurement then is used, not primarily for construction, but for comparison.

Figure Observation.

Measurement, in itself, may not fully describe the body: it should, where necessary, be amplified by the verbal description of any particular feature that cannot be accurately tabulated by measurement. To this end, it is necessary to be familiar with the various form types represented on the size card. The proportionate form of normal development should be taken as the standard, and all other types compared with this standard. The dimensions, distinguishing features, and characteristic posture of the main types may quite well be memorised. The student should train himself to detect where, and by what amount, any particular figure varies from the nearest charted type.

Obvious abnormalities or deformities are not difficult to detect and record, but there is a wide variety of peculiarities that demand training to detect—*e.g.*, dropped shoulder on one side only, hollow back, prominent chest, over- or under-developed seat, peculiarities of posture. The habit of the observation and description of such variations should be cultivated quite early in a pattern-drawing course. No detail that may go to the successful making of a pattern should be omitted or neglected.

Procedure.

(1) Measurements should be taken in a certain order; firstly, the lengths; secondly, the girths.

The girth measurements should be taken in their order, downwards from the upper girth to the lower dimension.

(2) Wherever possible, the measurement shall be made between one point on the body and another point on the body—*i.e.*, every measurement shall contribute definitely to

our assessment of the body. To begin or conclude a dimension at a variable or indefinite point (such as a garment length measured from a shoulder seam that may be placed anywhere within an inch) is to confuse our knowledge of the figure.

(3) The measures shall be not only taken, but set down, in a definite order. The position of any particular measurement in correct sequence of measures should indicate the dimension it actually refers to.

(4) In addition to the actual measurements any noticeable departure from the normal figure, or any deformity or abnormality, should be noted.

(5) The required style features should be set down clearly and in definite order, downwards from the upper part of a garment to the lower; the outside features of the garment should be described before those of the inside.

Method of Measurement.

The measurements for a trunk garment should be taken in the following order:—

Lengths:

(1) Nape to waist length, say 17 ins.

(2) Continue to hem say 29 ins.

(3) Spine to elbow say 20 1/2 ins.

(4) Continue to wrist bone 31 1/2 ins.

When taking (3) and (4) the upper arm should be at 90° to the back and the lower arm at 90° to the upper arm.

Girths:

(5) Girth of breast (on vest), say 37 ins.

(6) Girth of waist (on vest), say 34 ins.

(7) Girth of seat (on trousers), 39 ins.

Any special or check measurements will then be taken.

For a Vest, the two following measurements should be taken:

Nape to neck opening.

Nape to front point.

(Girth of neck, if necessary.)

Leg Garments. For trousers:

Lengths:

(1) Side length, waist to 1 in. above shoe welt, say 42 ins.

(2) Inside leg, from fork to 1 in. above shoe welt, say 31 1/2 ins.

(The trousers should be held fairly up to the fork when taking this measurement. This length assumes plain bottoms.)

Girths:

(3) Waist girth, say 33 ins.

(4) Seat girth, say 39 ins.

(5) Width of knee, 22 ins.

(6) Width of hem, 20 ins.

For breeches, the following *additional* lengths and girths should be taken:—

Lengths:

Knee to hollow.

Hollow to prominence of calf.

Calf to end of breeches leg.

Girths:

Knee (slightly bent).

Hollow.

Calf.

Bottom of continuation.

The height of the top above the waist-line has not been ascertained by direct measurement. In stock garments this amount will vary from 2 ins. to 2 3/4 ins. (plus seams and top turning), dependent on the height of the man. Work trousers are usually cut higher in the tops than garments for formal wear. In garments cut to special requirements, personal idiosyncracy will decide the matter.

Over-garments.

All types of over-garment patterns may be constructed from the basic girth measurements taken on the vest. Additions have to be made to these girth measures, and these extra amounts will vary with the type of garment. More will, of course, be required in the case of a loose-fitting raincoat than in a close-fitting garment for formal wear. These increases are for fitting and style.

An addition of 3/4 in. or 1 in. to the length of jacket sleeve, too, will have to be made, in order to secure that the over-sleeve will adequately cover the jacket sleeve.

Analysis of Measurements

Having taken the measurements correctly, they may be analysed, so that they may be understood better.

Two Types of Measure.

In the first place, it is necessary to distinguish between two different kinds of measurements. If a measure from the nape to the waist-line is taken, the distance from one distinct point of the body to another definite point is known. Other examples of this type of point-to-point measurement are, spine to elbow, spine to wrist-bone. The girth measures of breast, waist, seat, knee, hollow, are others of the same kind. These data do actually enable the student to visualise the type of figure being dealt with, whether tall, short, average, stout, thin, proportionate. Measurements in this category are definitely those which have to do with the size, shape, and proportion of the body: they may, therefore, be referred to as *body measurements.* When applied to the draft they form the anatomical basis of the pattern. The utmost value, therefore, attaches to these data, and the greatest care should be taken when collecting them.

Secondly, there are those other measurements that are concerned with the style of the garment. These include the lengths of vests, jackets, and over garments, the length of vest opening, length of lapel, widths of sleeve and trousers leg. A man's anatomical measurements may remain the same over a period of years; but his coats will be longer or shorter, from season to season, following the trend of style. His arm and leg may not change in girth, but his sleeve and trousers leg will vary in width with changes in fashion. These measurements are, of course, important, seeing that they embody the style or fashion-requirements of the garments. They may, therefore, be known as *style, or fashion, measurements.*

The measurements taken in respect of a customer will, then, fall into these two groups, and the student should early learn to distinguish between them. They have different applications and different values. Those of the body are basic, and do not change through the whim and caprice of fashion. They are concerned with the anatomical groundwork of the pattern, and are the measurements concerned in the working-out of any pattern system.

The measurements of the garment, on the other hand, reflecting as they do the season-to-season changes of fashion, are related, not to the physical basis of the pattern, but to the artistic side of pattern-drawing. The first set of measures fixes the few fitting-points and parts of the garment: the fashion measures are concerned with the length, width and position of all style features.

The drawing of a garment-pattern should, therefore, be regarded as:—

(1) Laying down a geometrical groundwork embodying the anatomical size and shape, and

(2) On this groundwork, the artistic drawing of the fashion features.

Both aspects are important; but they are different. Drafting, therefore, should, from the first, be regarded as a two-sided matter, employing two different sets of data.

Measurements Should be Comparable.

Measurements are taken in order that the cutter may visualise the figure, whether proportionate or otherwise; and if disproportionate, just exactly where the disproportion lies. The *relation between the different measurements* is the guide in this matter. If measurements stand in certain proportionate relationship to each other, then the designer recognises a proportionate figure. If the measures are not harmoniously related, a sense of discord, or disproportion, is obvious. The chief factor, then, in any comparison of measures is that they shall be comparable—*i.e.*, they shall be taken under identical conditions. For example, a nude body may be measured, and the girths compared. They will bear comparison because they have been taken under exactly identical conditions.

If, however, the body was clothed and the same girths taken again, but this time on the clothing, some important differences would be noted. Different parts of the body have more layers of clothing than others. The knee may have at most but one; the waist may have under-vest, shirt, perhaps a belt, and pants. If the relationship of the nude knee and nude waist were represented by as 15 to 34, the greater amount of clothing on the waist will have disturbed this ratio to as 15 1/4 is to 36. The same may be said of other parts of the body.

Take the gorge, or neck-girth, in the nude; then put on under-vest, shirt, collar, and tie. Find out the amount of increase and realise that any garment next put on has to fit comfortably over *the neck, plus these garments*. Go forward to add the waistcoat and the jacket; then count up the number of thicknesses of various materials which lie between the neck column and the outside collar. When these have been counted and checked, compare the bare neck-girth with the clothed neck-girth. The difference will cause surprise. There is here no question of drapery: each layer fits smoothly over the one underneath. But the increase in neck-girth of these snugly lying layers will be considerable.

The practical consideration is that this increase in girths has to be allowed for in making the pattern for the next garment worn over. Philosophers bid us study trends and tendencies in their ultimate catastrophes, and this approach may help us here. Assume a jacket or over-garment that fits well and is correctly balanced. Then, under this, put on a woollen muffler of normal type. This increases the neck-girth, and consequently the collar and shoulders no longer fit well; and the balance has been seriously disturbed by a radical picking-up of the front, without any compensating shortening behind.

The point made here, by taking a few examples, is capable of being strengthened by the obvious consideration that the different important girths of the body are clothed, *but not evenly clothed*, and that this clothing adds to the natural girths of the body, not evenly, but variously; this affects those garments with which tailors are concerned. An added complication is caused by wearing, at different seasons, different quantities of underclothing beneath the outer garments.

This consideration does not invalidate the work done by the anthropometrists who take their data from the unclothed body; but it certainly does modify their conclusions both as to girths and balance requirements. The men's tailor has to begin where the underwear manufacturer leaves off; just as the ladies' tailor has to clothe the figure created by the corsetiere; not the natural form of the woman.

Do not, however, conclude that the work of Wampen and his followers is of no practical use to the pattern-maker; it is, and will continue to be, of the greatest practical value, and should be the basis of every student's work. Anthropometry is the science of body measurement: the tailor is concerned with this, and with the modifications in size, shape, and balance caused by the underclothing which lies between the nude body and the outer garments.

Three Groups of Measurements

In any consideration of measurements deemed necessary to make the pattern, it will be seen that they fall into three groups:—

(*a*) measures of length;

(*b*) measures of girth;

(*c*) measures which include elements of both length and girth.

In respect of (*a*), the measurements which denote length, pure and simple, are applied to the pattern exactly as taken from the figure, without any addition or subtraction.

(*b*) Girth measurements must have an added tolerance; and this allowance will vary with the type of garment. Usually patterns are made of half the garment only, so that only half the total garment tolerance is used in the pattern. For example, in a vest, about 3/4 in. on the half garment is added over the nett half girths; in a jacket or similar garment, about 1 in. When garments cut to these patterns are finished, they will measure up about 1 1/2 ins. in the vest, and 2 ins. in the jacket, over the nett girth measurements. It has already been shown why these girth tolerances are necessary.

All garment-design systems, of whatever type, provide for these girth tolerances in the normal working-out of the system. Not all of them, however, show what the additional girth is needed for: nor do all provide the quantity by the same method. But in one way or another the tolerances for girth are made; and, broadly speaking, the amounts given above are those widely and normally adopted.

(*c*) Measurements which include elements of both length and girth tend to complicate this matter of tolerances. Yet the problem is fairly simple to grasp. Take as an example the middle-shoulder measurement, on which a scale is sometimes based. This measure begins on the spine, several inches below the nape, continues *across* the back, *down* the front of scye, under the arm, and thence diagonally back to the starting-point. This is no simple vertical or lateral measure, but one which contains elements of both. The scye-girth measure is another of the same kind. Even the nape to front-scye, or front breast-point, is in the same category. In fact, almost every measurement taken with the object of getting the mass-content of the shoulder has length and breadth so compounded, that *the result is a measurement of a third dimension*, neither entirely length, nor all breadth, but indicating *bulk, thickness*, or *mass*.

It will be seen that it is not easy to determine just what fractions of, say, the middle-shoulder measure can be marked as height or girth, but what is plain is that *some* tolerance must be added for whatever fraction *is* regarded as girth. These amounts are known: they have been determined accurately and scientifically. What is important for the student, however, is that he should realise that every system has correctly embodied these allowances. They were included before systematic construction became what it is today. They were empirical, but they were correct. The two main points to grasp here are, firstly, to realise that they are needed in the pattern, and, secondly, that every pattern-system takes them for granted and embodies them.

That the student may clear up this matter in a way that will impress the conclusions on his mind, let him take similar dimensions both *under* and *over* a garment. He should start with a simple girth, say the breast, and compare the two results. Then he may go on to a complex measurement, the scye girth on the shirt and on the jacket, or the middle-shoulder with the coat off and on. These comparisons will demonstrate the necessity for tolerances, and will show that they are embodied in every system by some more-or-less obvious method.

Senior students may then pass on to a discussion as to whether a tolerance should be a fixed amount or a percentage. To more than one craftsman it appears likely that system-makers, perhaps unwillingly, have allowed a fixed amount in respect of simple girth, but have allowed a percentage on measurements combining girth and length.

Ease in Fitting.

A further important point should be made here. It must not be supposed that an easy-fitting garment can be produced by merely adding something to the girth tolerance. In all reputable systems the agreed tolerances are as stated above and do not vary with the size of the garment. If an easier garment is needed it can be produced in only one way—namely, to increase the breast girth (and, of course, the waist and hips) by the amount of ease required, and to base the scale on the increased breast girth. For example, if an easy fitting 36-in. breast jacket is required, it would be fatal to reason than an 18-in. scale should be used, and a tolerance of, say, 2 ins. on the half-breast, used. The result of this wrong procedure would be to give a jacket in all fitting respects the same as a closely-cut 36-in., but with the *added* tolerance on the front of the garment. It cannot be too strongly stressed that the tolerance of 2 ins. on the jacket is, by the ordinary working out of any system, *distributed generally all over the girth of the garment.* The systematic amount only is distributed generally; but any excess of the amount must of necessity be deposited locally on the front of the garment. The simple facts to grasp here are:

(*a*) The girth of the garment, from centre back to centre front, is measured with the inch tape, and contains simply the half-breast plus the agreed tolerance.

(*b*) The position of the scye in the garment is not decided by applying any such simple direct measure, but is found by means of a scale quantity based on the nett half-breast measure; and no consideration of tolerances enters into this scale-fixing.

When it is pointed out that the scale is based on the actual breast girth, and not on the actual size of the garment, which is larger than the man, it should be understood quite literally to apply to all sorts of garments. Say that a jacket, a fitting overcoat, a sac over-garment, and a raglan raincoat were to be made for the same man. Assume that he is 38-in. breast girth on the vest.

Now, obviously, were all these garments cut to a scale of 19 ins. there would be some strange results. The jacket would fit over the vest and would follow the lines of the figure fairly closely. The fitting overcoat would follow the contours of the form, but as it had to fit over the jacket, it would need to be *cut larger in all its girths and in all sections of each girth.* Therefore, this would need to be cut to a 40-in. breast girth, with a 20-in. scale. The sac over-garment would, for style purposes, need to fit loosely, and therefore it would be cut to a 43-in. breast girth, with a 21 1/2-in. scale. The raglan raincoat should fit looser still, and would be cut to a 46-in. breast girth, with a 23-in. scale.

It should be noted that as the fitting overcoat is worn over the jacket, the breast measure on which the scale is based is assumed to be taken over the jacket. The sac over-garment could be worn over the fitting overcoat, and its breast measurement is assumed to be taken over the fitting overcoat. The raglan raincoat of cotton gaberdine could be worn over the total of the three previous garments, and is therefore correspondingly larger in girths. Now, arising out of this comparison there are the following points which must be made:—

(*a*) Any increase of girth for purposes of style should be regarded as mere increase of girth, *and should not be confused with the tolerances we have considered.*

(*b*) The scale in each case would be based on the indicated breast girth, and, in the normal working-out of the system, the *same tolerance would be automatically added. It is neither more nor less in the loose large raglan than in the snugly fitting jacket.*

Girth Tolerance and Scale.

Arising out of this, the question is sometimes put, that if a jacket cut for a 36-in. man, and having a 2-in. tolerance, measures 38 ins. from eye of buttonhole, across the garment to the neck of the button, a 38-in. garment has been produced, and yet a scale of only 18 ins. has been used. The 18 ins. is half the breast girth of the 36-in. man, and not half the breast girth of the 38-in. garment which the scale has automatically produced. The scale *is not* proportionately related to the girth of the garment it has produced, but *is* proportionately related to a measurement, which is always 2 ins. less than the garment. The answer to this question may be:—

Historically, patterns were made before pattern-making systems were evolved, and all systems were made from patterns which were found to fit certain figure types. Certain main fitting points were noticed to be in constant ratio to the *nett* breast measurement, and therefore when, in the gradual evolution of systems, designers began to fix these fittings points, they very naturally related them to the breast girth as measured, and not to the actual girth of the garment.

If it is objected that this explanation is too simple, it would be well to consider the evolution of the idea of system, or method, in pattern-making. Four generations ago patterns were produced without the aid of even a tape measure, for the good reason that such a piece of equipment did not then exist. Strips of parchment, notched in various places, indicated by the relative position of the notches, the various measurements. The customer's name was written on his own particular parchment strip, and it was retained as a permanent record.

If this line of thought be followed forward to the inch tape, then on to the first indication of the idea of proportion found in our trade—namely, the table of aliquot parts—then on to the graduated tape, which embodied the previous idea; then on still nearer the present, the graduated square; and, finally, the use of a "constant" in finding a suitable scale in cases of physical disproportion; it will be noted that the dominant measurement, all the time, was the dimension of the body without any addition.

Any scale, therefore, no matter how derived, would be a fraction of some one measurement, and it would be only natural to relate it to the size of the man, and not to the size of the garment.

APPLYING THE MEASUREMENTS TO THE PATTERN

THE necessary measures having been taken, analysed, and understood, how shall they be applied to the pattern? The method, or system, employed will depend very much on the student's training: his teacher may have insisted that one method, or system, was better than others. He may have been instructed in the mere mechanical working-out of a system, without much guidance in the principles he was applying. On the other hand, he may have been trained to understand the principles of fitting and draping by a teacher who regarded the principles involved as important as the method by which they are applied to the pattern.

(1) In the first place, the student should learn what a system can, and cannot, do. No system is entirely foolproof. Just as measurement demands intelligence and care, so the application of measures requires personal skill and an understanding of first principles. Any system, no matter how simple or mechanical, presupposes a man capable of using it intelligently.

(2) A system will not concern itself with style features, as such. So far as the trunk of the body is concerned, a system operates between the centre-back and centre-front construction lines. The construction of any particular type of

front1 is a matter of mere arithmetic and drawing: it belongs to the purely artistic side of the pattern. The run of a front; the size and shape of a lapel; the placing of pockets or other style features—these are not concerned with the anatomy of the figure. This will simplify the matter, and show, also, the part played by drawing, pure and simple, in the garment.

(3) There exists a traditional idea that every point and part of a garment may be fixed by a system. It is necessary to repeat that a system fixes only a few points, but these are important in that they are salient anatomical points. A system is a way of applying measures intelligently. Measures are taken on certain lines of the body. These lines are reproduced on the draft, and are called construction lines.

The length measurements will present no difficulty. The girths, plus tolerance, will raise no problem. If a rectangle be drawn, as *wide* as half the breast girth plus tolerance, and as *long* as the garment, then a start has been made. Suppressions and increments are usually effected by seams. In a normal figure the waist girth is less than the breast, but the seat girth is greater. Then on the waist-line some material is removed; on the seat-line material is added by overlaying parts. So far, progress is easy and does not make great demands. Then comes the fixing of points and parts in the neck and shoulder section. No direct measure has been taken for scye depth, yet a system will give this important point. No neck girth was measured, but a system will automatically give one.

The position of the front of scye has not been measured, yet it is placed by a system. No shoulder-height or scye-girth measurement has been made; yet here they are. How are these points fixed and parts placed? No direct measure was taken in respect of them.

They were placed by applying a *derived measurement*: a dimension derived from a reliable direct measure and standing in a certain proportionate relation to it.

The difficulty of taking reliable direct measures in the shoulder section is well recognised; it is deemed safer to use a dependable derived measure than an unreliable direct measure. These derived measures are fractions of a scale used for locating those points and parts for which no direct data were taken. This scale is taken from either the breast girth or the middle shoulder measure.

What, then, is a scale? Why is it derived from one of these two dimensions? How is it applied to the normal figure? What happens when disproportion is met? These questions need to be answered; and they may be taken in logical order.

A scale must, to be a scale at all, be derived from a measurement that is proportionately related to the parts which are to be constructed by the scale. These parts lie in the shoulder section of the pattern.

The *length measurements*, as such, are not proportionately related to the shoulder section, and so may be ruled out as bases for a scale.

The *girth measurements* of *breast, waist,* and *seat* are always taken. Of these three, the waist is most variable. When weight begins to increase it is usually, in the male, deposited on the front waist to a much greater degree than elsewhere. Fat is seldom found anywhere but on the soft parts of the body, where there is no bone structure immediately beneath.

It is possible to find a very wide range of waist girths to any given breast girth—*e.g.*, a 40-breast figure may have a waist girth of 32 ins., or 45 ins., or any unit between. Such a variable and unreliable measure may not be used as a basis for a scale.

The *seat girth* depends on the greater or lesser development of the gluteal muscles. These are not related to the size and development of the shoulder mass. The seat measure will not help in finding a scale.

There remains the *breast-girth dimension.* This is the nearest basic girth to the shoulder section, and its size and development do give a reliable index to the development of the shoulders. It is least liable to variation or change from occupational and accidental causes. It affords the truest index to the development of the skeleton form.

The *middle-shoulder measure is*, as has been pointed out, of use for comparison with the other measurements, but it does not offer the reliability needed for scale-finding. It gives not only the size of the shoulder-mass, but also its position. The forward position of the arms, in the semi-stooping or slouching figure, will increase the measurement; while in the erect figure, with arms braced back, the measurement will decrease. Two figures, of the same *size* of shoulder, but one erect and the other slouching, will give two different measures. The advocates of shoulder-measure scales claim this as an advantage, but this is to be doubted. The normal sectional systems of drafting assume proportion, in one of its several variations, and any measure which is bound to register *attitude* as well as *size* may not be taken as a reliable basis for a scale which deals with size only.

(1) Direct-Measure Systems.

A scale is applied to a pattern only when a *sectional system* is used: *direct-measure systems* cannot employ a scale.

In a direct-measure system direct measures only are used. No scale quantities enter into the method. The figure for which such a system is used is regarded as neither proportionate nor disproportionate. These terms, and the idea for which they stand, are not considered by direct measures. The figure is regarded on its merits as an individual form, represented solely by the measurements taken, and having size and shape peculiar to itself. The systems using only direct measurements depend for their success on the accurate taking of short measures in the shoulder section, and in adding an appropriate tolerance in each case. The difficulty of correctly taking short measures, the computing of correct tolerances, and of applying the measures to the pattern, are generally acknowledged.

(2) Sectional Systems.

These systems are not *entirely* sectional in operation, seeing that direct measures are taken and used. The main distinction between (1) and (2), however, is that in (1) all points are found by direct measurement while in (2) a *few* points are located by direct measures, and other important sectional points and parts are found by the use of inferred measures, or scale quantities. These systems definitely commit themselves to the idea of physical proportion, because the points located by scale quantities are assumed to be proportionate to the measurements on which the scale is based. This is not an argument in favour of either of these main methods of construction: all that needs to be stressed here is that once a scale is employed, the idea of physical proportion has been conceded and adopted.

Sectional systems themselves fall into two groups:—

(*a*) Where the scale is based on a shoulder measurement, usually the middle shoulder. A fraction of this measure (two-thirds more or less) is taken as a scale, and quantities of this scale are then employed to locate points in respect of which no direct measurements have been taken.

The exponents of this method state that, as the shoulder of the coat is the section in which the control of the whole garment, both in the shoulder itself where it fits, and below the scye where it may possibly drape, is centred, then a measurement denoting the content of the shoulder should be regarded as of first importance and the scale accordingly based upon it.

Wampen, on the other hand, indicated a difficulty:—

"Diagonal measures, such as those from the shoulder, though they are sometimes taken, cannot be much relied on. The uncertainty of obtaining the correct diagonal measure is owing solely to the naturally continuous changing of the physical position of the figure" (*Anthro.*, p. 10).

It should, further, be stated that the shoulder is so liable to serious forms of over- and under-development due to occupational and other causes, and is, therefore, unrelated in size to other parts of the trunk, as to render it somewhat uncertain as a quantity on which to base a scale.

By this method of construction, then, all the points fixed by means of a scale are assumed to be related, in certain known proportions, to the shoulder measure from which the scale is derived. The method is therefore proportionate and the standard of proportion is a shoulder measurement.

(*b*) The other group of sectional systems using a few direct measures and for the rest, inferred sectional measurements, is based on the breast-girth measurements. A fraction (1/2 more or less) of this girth is taken and used as a scale, quantities of which are used to locate points in respect of which no direct measurements have been taken. This method is commended by its advocates on the ground that the breast girth, of all the measurements, best reflects the general development of the trunk and the relationship of its parts, and may therefore be safely taken as the norm or denominator of the trunk. It is further urged that the breast girth is not so liable to over- or under-development from occupational and other causes; and finally that the measurement is a simple one involving girth only, not two dimensions, girth and length, as does the middle shoulder.

Again, although it is not generally put forward by breast-scale advocates, there seems to be general agreement that more is known of the relationship of the various parts of the trunk to the breast girth, and for this reason greater accuracy may be expected in the use of breast scales.

This method, too, assumes proportion and the breast girth as the standard.

Now, most systems use two sorts of dimensions—namely, those of height and those of girth. In the proportionate figure there is a harmony of the two. For the proportionate figure, therefore, it is possible for a scale derived from a girth quantity to be applied to height—*e.g.*, for a scale fraction to be used for depth of scye. In figures where the proportionate relationship between height and girth is disturbed by excess of either quantity, the scale based on a girth dimension cannot be safely used for height quantity. It will be obvious, therefore, that when only one scale—*i.e.*, one based on a girth—is used, the system assumes a proportionate form. Where any modification is made in the system, in respect of greater or less, height than proportionate, then we have, by implication, two scales in operation, namely, one for girth and one for height.

Wampen treated the proportionate form as a harmony which permitted height and girth to synchronise in one scale. So far did he take this idea in the direction of simplicity that he argued the possibility of building a complex garment structure from the simplest and most meagre data: ". . . the following measures are those requiring chief attention. First, the entire height of the figure, second, the thoracial circumference, third, the size of the waist."

"This, however, is certain and assured by very extensive experience that if the proportions of the different kinds of form of the human figure are once known and perfectly understood, then the smallest amount of measurement from the figure, combined with these proportions, constitutes the most easy and certain method to follow" (*Anthro.*, p. 10).

The garment designer, in a wholesale house, does, as a matter of common practice, produce a garment pattern for a "regular" size by taking a breast girth or shoulder measure and assuming that other measurements are proportionate to that quantity. In long, short and stout sizes, too, this assumption can be made.

Having seen the relation of a scale to measurement and systems of various kinds, it will be possible to consider how a scale is related to a garment during construction.

Without discussing any of the *general* definitions of a scale, we may define a garment scale as a proportionate quantity of a governing representative dimension, used to proportionately locate the various points and parts of a garment for which no direct measurements have been taken. A garment, proportionate in all the parts located by scale, will then be produced.

The parts located by a scale will vary as between systems: the general effect of scale-working, however, no matter from what governing dimension it may be derived, is to give:—

An adequate shoulder,

A correctly placed scye, laterally and vertically,

A correct gorge.

All systems using a scale quantity for scye depth will give a balance suitable for a proportionate figure. Assuming that the proportionate person of normal development stands in a certain way—*i.e.*, not stooping or over-erect, but normally upright—the use of a scale quantity will secure this "proportionate balance".

This, then, is the principle underlying all sectional systems, and the general success of most methods embodying it would appear to argue the correctness of principle and method. Ideally, and in logical extension, a perfect and complete knowledge of human proportion would enable a pattern to be made from one dimension only, all other measurements being found by inference. All sectional systems, therefore, take the proportionate body for granted and any disproportion is provided for by modification of system.

When the student has learned to differentiate between

(*a*) those parts of a pattern located by direct measure,

(*b*) those parts of a pattern derived by scale quantities, and

(*c*) those parts of a pattern which reflect some disproportion and are modification of (*b*),

then he is on the way to understanding the anatomical elements of pattern making.

The Use of a Scale in Disproportion.

Variations from proportion fall into several groupings and, to illustrate the use of a scale in disproportion, three common types may be taken:

(1) Disproportion of height and girth.

(2) Disproportion of thigh girth and seat girth.

(3) Disproportion of shoulder content and breast girth.

(1) Disproportion of Height and Girth: Men.

The height quantity most frequently taken as a fraction of a girth scale is the depth of scye. Most other height quantities are found by direct measurement.

The position that arises is that the student is instructed to fix his breast line at half-scale, or perhaps a sixth of scale plus a constant quantity, below the nape line. He thus gives the same scye depth to two men of the same breast girth, but of a foot difference in height. Which, of course, is neither sound practice nor intelligent theory.

It has been noted that the fixing of a height quantity—for example, the depth of scye—by taking a fraction of a scale based on girth, assumes a relationship between height and girth, and that the relationship is proportionate.

If half the breast scale is used to locate the scye base, then its vertical position would vary only with a change in breast girth. The assumption, therefore, is that the height harmonises with the breast girth—*i.e.*, that the form is proportionate or regular.

The quantity of scye depth, from the nape to the armpits, is indisputably a part (approximately one-eighth) of the total height of the figure. If half the working scale is used for this height quantity, every increase or decrease in girth will assume a corresponding increase or decrease in height. A breast girth of 38 ins. giving a scale of 19 ins. will locate the scye depth at 9 1/2 ins. below the nape. (This 9 1/2 ins. is assumed to be the *contour length* of the nape to breast section, not necessarily the vertical height, and is *associated with the regular figure of normal posture.*) For a 40-in. breast figure the scale would give a scye depth of 10 ins., a 34-in. girth would give 8 1/2 ins.

These differences in scye depth certainly assume that any increase or decrease in girth is accompanied by an increase or decrease in height. But the whole of the difference cannot be accounted for by height. A taller man will, of course, need a deeper scye; height makes its special demand. But girth, too, has to be considered. If a man maintains his height unaltered, but increases in breast girth, that girth increase will demand a deeper scye. The deposit of fleshy tissue under the arm will lower the actual position of the armpit. (A similar point arises in trousers construction. The height of a man will remain unchanged while increase in his girths is accompanied by a lowering of the fork by the deposit of tissue in that part. The inside leg measurement is, therefore, less, and the body rise greater, than before the girths increased.)

We, therefore, reach this position:—

(*a*) increase in *height* alone, unaccompanied by girth increase, demands a deeper scye;

(*b*) increase in *girth* alone, without any increase in height necessitates a deeper scye;

(*c*) increases in both *height and girth* at the same time demand a greater scye depth.

The working of a normal scale assumes the double increase of (c):

What, then, should be done in the cases of (a) *and* (b)?

Certain factors will help here; and they are embodied in the idea of *the use of two scales*, one for the girths and one for the height quantities, in one pattern. It is generally accepted that an inch of increase in height, alone, necessitates the deepening of the scye by one-eighth of that amount. It is also generally agreed that an inch of increase in girth, alone, requires the deepening of the scye by one eighth of an inch.

Where both *height and girth* increase by 1 in. each, a quarter of an inch more of scye depth will be needed. (What is said of increase applies, inversely, to decreases.) An inch of girth increase in the breast girth will result in half an inch increase in the scale and a quarter of an inch increase in the scye depth quantity (half scale). It is seen, then, that the normal working of a scale assumes that every inch of girth increase is automatically accompanied by an extra inch of height. This in many instances is a sound assumption, but the exceptions are sufficiently numerous and important to necessitate the adoption of special methods of variation.

An accepted standard should first be fixed. The regular standard of 5 ft. 8 ins. and 38 ins. breast girth with a scye depth of 9 1/2 ins. is recommended; it has become the norm of wholesale pattern design, and appears to meet the requirements of the industry. By making suitable additions to, or subtraction from, this standard, in respect of variations of height or girth, or both, a satisfactory result is obtained.

Examples:—

(*a*) *Height variation only:*

(1) Height 6 ft., breast 38 ins.

Standard scye depth 9 1/2 ins. plus 1/2 in. for greater height = 10 ins. scye depth.

(2) Height 5 ft. 5 ins., breast 38 ins.

Standard scye depth 9 1/2 ins. minus 3/8 in. for less height = 9 1/8 ins. scye depth.

(*b*) *Girth variation only:*

(1) Height 5 ft. 8 ins. breast 41 ins.

Standard scye depth 9 1/2 ins. plus 3/8 in. for greater girth = 9 7/8 ins. scye depth.

(2) Height 5 ft. 8 ins., breast 34 ins.

Standard scye depth 9 1/2 ins. minus 1/2 in. for less girth = 9 ins. scye depth.

(*c*) *Height and girth variation:*

(1) Height 5 ft. 10 ins., breast 37 ins.

Standard scye depth 9 1/2 ins. plus 1/4 in. for greater height minus 1/8 in. for less girth = 9 5/8 ins. scye depth.

(2) Height 5 ft. 4 ins., breast 39 ins.

Standard scye depth 9 1/2 ins. minus 1/2 in. for less height plus 1/8 in. for greater girth = 9 1/8 ins. scye depth.

Height and Girth: Women's Garments.

Depth of Scye.

The same principles apply as in men's garments: the application is, however, a little different.

The depth of scye would be increased or decreased 1/8 in. from a given standard for every inch of variation in height. For every inch of variation in girth, 1/16 in. would be allowed. This variation in girth allowance is only half of that for the male figure. The reason is that when weight increase takes place in the female form, the tissue is not deposited in the armpit to anything like the same extent as in the male. In this respect, the student should note that when a woman begins to put on weight, the upper arm, including biceps, triceps, and deltoids, may increase in a marked degree, without the scye girth measure showing anything near a corresponding increase.

A standard scye depth should first be fixed. Assume that a woman of 5 ft. 5 ins. in height and 36 ins. breast girth requires a scye depth of 8 1/2 ins.

Examples:

(*a*) Height 5 ft. 8 ins., 34 ins. breast girth.

8 1/2 ins. standard, plus 3/8 in. for greater height, minus 1/8 in. for less girth = 8 3/4 ins. scye depth.

(*b*) Height 5 ft. 4 ins., 42 ins. breast girth.

8 1/2 ins. standard, minus 1/8 in. for less height, plus 3/8 in. for greater girth = 8 3/4 ins. scye depth.

(Whether this standard scye-depth quantity will suit every type of garment production is not argued: it is given as illustrating a principle and a method. The standard should be fixed by the individual designer with the desired result in mind.)

Variations for Height other than Size-depth.

In the regular figure of 5 ft. 8 ins. height, the trousers leg length is computed at 32 1/2 ins., the forearm of sleeve at 18 ins., the nape to waist length at 17 ins.: dependent and secondary measurements are derived from these main dimensions. The waist length and the forearm sleeve are *approximately* one-quarter of the total height and the leg measure as one-half. For every inch of variation of height above or below the standard an increase or decrease will be made in these sectional measurements: waist length 1/4 in., forearm sleeve 1/4 in., leg 3/8 in.

These variations obviously do not hold good in the stout and corpulent forms.

Variations for Height: Women

In the *W*1 figure of 5 ft. 5 ins. height, the forearm of sleeve is accepted as 17 ins., and the nape to waist as 15 ins. These measures are nearly one-quarter of the total height. For every inch of variation of height above or below the standard an addition or subtraction of 1/4 in. will, therefore, be made in respect of these measures.

(2) Disproportion of Thigh and Seat.

In the majority of leg garment systems where the seat girth is used as a measurement on which to base a scale, the fork quantities of topside and underside (really *one* quantity divided by a seam) are not found by a direct measurement, but are assumed to be a definite fraction of the seat girth. Fork quantity is thigh drapery; therefore the girth of the thigh is assumed to be proportionate to the seat girth. This undoubtedly holds good in all proportionate bodies of normal form. In cases, however, where the trunk dimensions increase by such an amount as to be disproportionate, the normal ratio of thigh to seat does not hold good. In bodies where the waist has developed to corpulence it will be found that this deposit of tissue, which is at its maximum at the front waist, is also reflected in the seat girth. In such cases the thigh will be relatively smaller to the seat girth than it would be in a proportionate figure. Fork quantity, in garments for corpulent men, therefore, will need to be less.

To effect this, a constant is used to steady and restrain the scale. The constant will represent the seat girth of a man who has grown in size to the point when disproportion (corpulency) has begun to develop. A figure round 42 ins. seat would be appropriate. The mean of the constant and of the actual seat girth would give a scale below the amount of half actual seat, but above the scale of half of the constant; and would give a satisfactory quantity of fork for all sizes of corpulent figure.

Example:—

Waist 52 ins.; seat 46 ins.

Scale equals 46 ins. actual s.g.,1 plus 42 ins. constant, equals 88 ins./2 equals 44 ins. mean s.g. equals 22 ins. scale.

For a proportionate man, however, of 46 ins. seat, the scale would be half seat girth equals 23 ins. scale.

(*Note.*—The practice of using thigh scales in leg garment construction is not usual. One well-known designer, however, has very successfully used such scales for a long period.)

(3) Disproportion of Shoulder Content and Breast Girth.

The application of scale fractions gives a shoulder proportionate to a breast girth in proportionate sizes. When there exists any abnormality of size, the normal relation between these scale-fixed parts and breast girth breaks down, and a scale that will reflect the abnormality must be found. In corpulency, the excess of tissue at the front waist is reflected in the breast girth, which has developed disproportionately to the shoulder. Relative to the breast girth the shoulder is small: therefore the scale which constructs the shoulder must be smaller than half the breast. A constant is again used here. The constant will be the breast girth of a man in the upper reaches of size, but not yet corpulent; say 42 ins. breast girth.

The mean of this constant and of the actual breast girth will give a scale below the amount of half breast; but above a scale of half the constant. By using such a scale an adequate shoulder will result.

Example:—

Breast 48 ins.; waist 53 ins.

Scale equals 48 ins., actual b.g.2 plus 42 ins. constant equals 90 ins./2 equals 45 ins. mean b.g. equals 22 1/2 ins. scale.

(For a *proportionate* man of 48 ins. breast girth the scale would be half breast girth equals 24 ins. scale. He would, however, be very big!)

Had a scale of half the breast been used, the following defects would have resulted:

Shoulder too "straight".

Back too wide.

Front too narrow.

Scye too deep.

Scye too large.

Scye too forward.

Gorge larger than required.

Graduation and Scales.

The use of a constant to modify a scale used in the construction of shoulder and fork in corpulent forms is illustrated in an improved type of graduated tape used more commonly some years ago than today. It will be recalled that a normal set of tapes contained all sizes from 12 ins. to 24 ins. or 25 ins. inclusive, and that from the 18 ins. standard unit the ratio of increase and decrease was constant and regular, through all sizes. Within the range of proportionate sizes these tapes gave reliable results in sectional systems; as, of course, they should, seeing they assumed a regular ratio of increase in all derived dimensions.

In the case of corpulent figures, however, where the shoulder and fork were disproportionately small compared with the breast and seat measures respectively, the use of tapes which maintained a constant unitary increase in the larger sizes was not satisfactory: they produced relative parts that were too large.

An improved set of tapes, however, was produced, in which all sizes over 20 ins. were subject to a slowing-up of unitary increase, thus reflecting the needs of construction more accurately than did the older type of tape. (The opposite possibly applied to all tape sizes under 15 ins., but this point cannot be definitely checked.) The principle of the use of a constant was thus adopted and used to modify scales for disproportionate figures.

It will, therefore, be seen that graduated tapes were graduated scales, and they made a not unsuccessful attempt to make arithmetic march with, and reflect, physical development. While graduated tapes are little used today as a mechanical aid to pattern-making, the principle they embody is more widely applied than ever.

The Use of a Constant.

The use of a constant to modify a scale meets the following position: where the shoulder and breast are out of basic proportionate ratio, one of two methods must be adopted; *either* the scale must be reduced and the scale quantities maintained in their original notation, *or* the scale kept at half the breast for all sizes and the scale quantities progressively reduced as size increases. Either course is logical, but the latter course would reduce the construction of a pattern to a task demanding the most abstruse calculations, and would end in chaos. The scale must, then, be progressively reduced, and the use of a suitable constant enables this to be done satisfactorily.

Scales so derived do, at least, regard the shape of a figure as of equal importance to its size, or, to put the same principle in a somewhat different way, growth (*i.e.*, size; the deposit of tissue) and development (*i.e.*, the shape resulting from growth) are both to be considered when finding a scale.

Balance in Abnormal Figures.

It has been previously said that the use of a scale gives a garment balance suitable for a proportionate figure. Any special balance requirements, as, for example, corpulency in men, will have to be regarded as outside the scope of a scale. To illustrate: up to a certain point of front development, the working of a scale will give an appropriate nape to centre-front-waist measurement. After that point, however, balance length will need to be provided over and above the amount provided by scale working.

There are, then, obvious limitations to the application of scale quantities to pattern-making, and these limitations are the various types of disproportion and abnormality met with. What does matter, however, is to know the principles involved and the limits of their application: both lie, it would appear, in a fuller understanding of those two much-used terms, proportion and disproportion.

Scale-finding for Women's Garments.

The principles so far set forth in these notes have been argued from, and based on, the male figure. The basic fitting points of both men's and women's trunk garments are so similar in location that it may be useful to extend the discussion to scale-finding for women's garments. From the purely sartorial point of view, the principles concerned do not recognise difference of sex; but merely variations of shape and size.

A correct scale for the construction of a pattern for a woman's garment will need to take into account the local development of bust. Wampen defined the relation between breast and bust in the uncorseted body and stressed that bust should be regarded as a local glandular development and not as related to the structure of the trunk (*Anthro.*, p. 57, Pl. VII, Fig. B).

At a time when bust girths are widely used to denote garment sizes it would be useful to re-examine the "sinus of bosom" or bust difference, and to ask what this amounts to in different form types and sizes, in normal and abnormal figures. If, for example, the difference in a size 8 is 1 in. and in the larger out-sizes as much as 4 1/2 ins., what will be the difference in intermediate sizes of normal form? And further, how far is this bust difference, which at its maximum is local, reflected in adjacent parts? It is certainly not reflected in any growth or development of the general bone structure of the thorax; it may, however, in its excess of size over breast indicate some slight general deposit of tissue over the trunk generally.

It is noted that the conclusions of anatomy and anthropometry are unlikely to be of use here; the data of the uncorseted body are not very helpful when considering the corseted trunk. Further, the conclusions reached by earlier systematic writers who based their work on a radically different corsetry cannot today be accepted without re-examination. Having accepted the position that *a scale should arithmetically represent the physical growth and development of a figure*, it will be necessary to see how the proportions of the female form have altered.

So far as garment design is concerned, the effects of corsetry cannot, at any time, be regarded as settled for long. In the space of only a few years the vogue has changed from the high, full bust, wasp waist and generous hip to the flat boyish torso, unrestrained waist and lean hips. And it should be borne in mind that every system maker has the form-type of his time in mind when laying down the premises from which he argues his points of system.

This relation of form to system may be illustrated by comparing the conclusions of Hopkins with those now available. In his *Twentieth Century System of Ladies' Garment Cutting* appears a table of relative proportions which relates to the early years of this century and which reflects the figures of the period. In the table below I select two representative, modern figures of 34 ins. and 38 ins. breast respectively, and afford a comparison with two figures, of similar breast girth, of a generation ago. Average height is assumed in each case.

	Breast.	Waist	Seat	Scye Depth.	Waist Length.	Scye Circum.	Shoulder Measure.
Hopkins . .	34	23	40	7½	15½	15	24
1941 . .	34	26	36	8	15½	16½	25½
Hopkins . .	38	26	43	8¼	16	16¼	26⅝
1941 . .	38	30	40	8¾	16	17½	29

Analysis.

(The breast girth is the same in each case and gives a standard.)

(*a*) The nape to waist measure has not altered.

(*b*) The waist girth has increased.

(*c*) The hip girth has decreased.

(*d*) The scye is deeper.

(*e*) The shoulder measure has increased.

(*f*) The scye circumference has increased.

The shape of the trunk has changed, due to altered ratios of breast, waist and hip girths. The shoulder section shows an increase in size. The position of the arm socket in the body is *relatively* (and perhaps actually) more forward.

There is every reason for assuming that the earlier figures would show a substantial bust development over the breast measure. The modern forms, of the sizes indicated, do not show more than 34 ins. one inch, and 38 ins. an inch and three-quarters bust development. The shape of the trunk, therefore, is quite different, not only dimensionally, but in the relation of the arms to the trunk and in the development and more forward placing of the shoulder.

While only two sizes are dealt with, it should be stressed that the comparisons are in respect of normal, representative figures. Similar comparisons have been made in a range of sizes, and the conclusions above apply equally. Even in the outsize group, where little variation was expected over a period of, roughly, thirty years, the differences were striking.

There is, also, a generally accepted opinion that the average height of Englishwomen is greater than it was fifty years ago. Definite figures, placing the matter beyond doubt, do not seem to be available. The most reliable statistics examined appear reasonably convincing that a life of greater freedom and physical activity has added an inch to their average stature over a half century.

The modern figure approaches more nearly the proportions of the uncorseted trunk than did the form type common thirty years ago. Where the figure of a generation ago may be described as a *distorted* variant of the natural figure, the function of modern corsetry seems to be *control*, rather than distortion. (Those wishing to study the effect of extreme distortion by corsetry should read Prof. Flower's *Fashion in Deformity* and Luke Limner's *Madre Natura*.)

It is plain that the ratios to each other of the three main girth measures have never been static for more than a few years together; and any methods of waist suppression or hip increase based on one type of figure would not be found applicable to another. Sufficient has been said to indicate that the greater demands on the designer in the mantle trade arise as much from anatomical changes as from continuous fashion movements. Constructional formulæ, based on a given figure, are no sooner published than a change of vogue in form renders them unreliable.

In the uncorseted figure, the size of bust very largely determines its position: no generally correct position for all sizes can be accepted. The lifting of the bust, by corsetry, had the effect of increasing the breast girth, and it is this that concerns us when considering scales. It is therefore suggested:

(*a*) That where the figure has no appreciable development of bust and is of the flat, boyish type, a scale of half the breast will be appropriate. The breast measurement will represent the basic bone structure of the trunk: the breast measure of this undeveloped type is as much a "skeleton" measurement as is that of the young man.

(*b*) Where, however, bust development has resulted in a larger than basic breast girth, the shoulder is regarded as not having developed in size at the same rate as has the breast. A scale of half the breast would give a too-large shoulder and gorge, with a too-forward and too-deep scye. A constant should, therefore, be used in conjunction with the breast measurement; and the scale based on the mean of the actual and the constant. The constant should be the assumed breast girth of an adult figure in which bust development has not yet appreciably begun: say 32 ins.

(*a*) Undeveloped figure. Breast 34 ins.; bust 35 ins.

Scale equals half breast measurement equals 17 ins. scale.

(*b*) Developed figure. Breast 37 ins.; bust 39 1/2 ins.

Scale 37 ins. actual b.g. plus 32 ins. constant equals 69 ins./2 equals 34 1/2 mean breast girth equals 17 1/4 ins. scale.

This mean breast girth is assumed to be the dimension to which the actual shoulder is proportionate

1 S.B., D.B. Link, etc. 791 *W* = women's (the standard size).1 Seat girth.

2 Breast girth.

GARMENT SHAPE

The Uses of Seams.

THE materials of which clothing is made are woven fabrics, made to various widths (single or double) and in pieces of varying length. It is obvious that these materials will be flat and without shape. To produce a shapely garment from a shapeless fabric is the basic problem in all garment design.

The normal method of creating shape in a garment is by the use of the seam. The more draped and less fitting a garment is, the fewer seams are required—*e.g.*, the cape. The more fitting and less draped the garment, the more seams will be needed—*e.g.*, the bodice. The chief function of the seam, then, is to create shape.

The surface of the body is not flat: it represents a series of greater or lesser concavities and convexities. The fabrics used to clothe the body are not woven in convex or concave shapes, but flat. The problem, therefore, is, how to so arrange the seams of a garment that the required shape is created.

The problem is modified by the following considerations:—

(1) Few garments fit the body in every part. Even in those parts of the body where a garment is required to fit, the fit is not exact and absolute—*i.e.*, it does not "fit like a skin". The fact that garments may be correctly described as "fitting" or "semi-fitting" recognises degrees of closeness of fit. Even in the control section of a body garment the fit may be "close", "easy", "generous", etc. The term "fitting", therefore, is capable of application in varying degrees. In this connection the references to "Fitting and Draping" should be revised.

(2) *Manipulation of the fabric* may be regarded as a possible alternative to the seam in the infusion of shape into the garment. By manipulation is meant the stretching, shrinking, or drawing-in of any part of the garment so that it is more nearly shaped to the surface of the body.

When garments were made throughout by craftsmen it was possible to ensure that all the required manipulation was secured. It was, indeed, in this shaping and manipulation that the essence of craftsmanship lay. Sectional manufacture, however, has meant standardised manufacture, and it is not possible to secure any great amount of manipulation by the factory method of production. Whereas under the craft system of making clothing less was demanded of the cutter and more of the tailor, under the factory system little is demanded of the operator beyond standardised operation, but much is demanded of the .designer. He must endeavour to secure as many as possible of the effects of manipulation by means of a careful placing of seams. What the old-time tailor achieved by his manipulative skill must now be attempted by the designer.

As an example of the alternatives of the use of a seam, or manipulation, the back shoulder may be taken as simple and typical. The shaping of the back of the coat to fit the back of the figure may be done in two ways: firstly, by easing excess length of back on to the front at the shoulder-seam, and, secondly, by using a panel seam from which a moderate suppression is taken from nothing at the blade prominence to, say, 3/4 in. at the shoulder. In each case shape would be secured and the garment will be more nearly fitting than if neither of these alternatives had been adopted.

(3) Seams (of various kinds) are frequently used in women's garments for purposes of style. In men's garments seam placings are as static and conventional as men's fashions; in all descriptions of women's wear the seam is often employed to secure fashion effects that would be difficult to obtain by other means. A seam placement, therefore, may be dictated by the vogue of the moment; but the skilful designer will turn these fashion seams into means of creating "line" and shape that would be otherwise impossible. Two simple examples are: (1) the use of the seams afforded by inset vertical panels in coats and jackets, and (2) the use

of the pintuck in "rayed" groupings to create shape at the front- and back-neck of dresses.

(4) There are few "lateral" seam placings at the disposal of the designer. The conventional arrangements are practically all vertical. So long as an appearance of slenderness is desired by women, so long will the designer be committed to vertical arrangements. The yoke, in shoulder and hip, is perhaps the notable exception; but even the yoke is seldom without its transition lines. In dresses, horizontal or diagonal seams may be introduced in order to obtain flared effects. It will be seen, therefore, that lateral seam placings afford but few and small opportunities of creating shape.

The new fashions of each season bring some modification of previous seam arrangements. In those garments where good design is of first importance, seam placings are so constantly changing that general rules, beyond those considered above, would be of little value. *Opportunity should be made, in all practical work, of using all possible seams in a drawn pattern to secure the shape-effects desired.*

(5) Men's garments are almost entirely designed with vertical seam placings. The first reason is that the suggestion of height conveyed by the vertical seam is desirable. The second is that seams are not used for decorative purposes, in men's attire, so the seam becomes solely a means of giving shape.

The Shape of a Garment.

As to the actual shape produced in a garment, there was no clear-cut line to be drawn between the functions of the retail-bespoke cutter and of the craftsman tailor. In those garments where shapeliness was desired, much manipulation and handling were necessary. Various pieces of the garment were drawn-in in one part and, possibly, stretched in another by means of the iron. If one considers how manipulation entered into the shaping of, say, a pair of riding breeches, one becomes conscious that the art of breeches-making lay in the close co-operation of cutter and tailor. Much shape was imparted in the cutting-room, more was infused into the garments by the tailor who made them. That passing method of production demanded a very high standard of craftsmanship. Many pairs of breeches are today made by the older method, and superb garments are the result, but a large majority of the total output are made under a system of factory production, where the standard of manipulative skill is very low, or absent altogether. Whatever shapeliness, therefore, is required in the garment, must be procured by means of seams and other low-skilled devices. One wholesale producer put the matter succinctly when he said, "To-day the garments have to be made in the cutting-room." It was his way of summing up a system of garment manufacture where the actual making has become merely a series of mechanised operations, from which craft skill is practically eliminated.

FIG. 7.

In such a system of production, then, the designer of the pattern is required to impart to the garment whatever degree of shapeliness is required. And, even so, it is a matter of common experience that a low grade of make will nullify the intentions of the most skilful designer.

To take a further example, the illustration of the parts of a morning coat is given, showing how the shape of the body is imparted to the various parts. Shaped seams, drawing-in, stretching, easing-on, shrinking—all these methods are used to gain the ends of shape or form.

The amount of form, or modelling, secured by shaped seams will be obvious (Fig. 7).

Shape created by drawing-in is marked by 2.

Shape created by stretching is marked by 3.

Shape created by easing-on is marked by 4.

Shape created by shrinking is marked by 5.

Thus the main problem of design is presented—namely, how best to arrange for flat, shapeless pieces of material to fit a body surface that is not flat or shapeless.

It will have been noticed that where any degree of manipulation is introduced, some of the most vital fitting points in the flat design are disturbed by half an inch, and often more. To illustrate, a shoulder was designed on the flat and then manipulated into shape. The following changes from the flat position were made:—

(1) Neck-point moved upwards and forwards by straining out the gorge and shoulder.

(2) The front has been lifted upwards and forwards by bridling and by a gorge dart.

(3) The over-shoulder measure has been increased by stretching out over the shoulder bone.

(4) The line, front-of-scye-to-neck-point, has been shortened by shrinking.

Now, all these are legitimate and desirable methods of moulding a flat piece of material to a part of the thorax that is by no means flat. But it does appear evident that after all these things have been done, the positions of points considered vital have been seriously disturbed. If they were right in the flat, they are wrong after manipulation. If, on the other hand, differing quantities and qualities of manipulation (determined by the type of make) were taken into account by various system-makers, then there is no basis for comparison between them, but only a settled, but unspoken, conviction that the success of any garment system depends on the method of make to which the garment will be submitted.

This was pointedly emphasised when a well-known designer, whose salary ran into four figures, laid down the draft of a lounge jacket before a Northern Society. The actual draft was, by permission, used within a few days by the then President, who was a merchant tailor, for a customer of the given dimensions. It produced a very bad coat indeed. Had the coat been made by sectional workers in a factory it would have turned out well; but it was subjected to a better, *though very different*, type of craft make; hence the trouble. Any given system, therefore, must of necessity imply a certain type of make. This point has been intentionally laboured because, while it is vaguely known that the type of make does necessitate important changes in traditional design, it does not appear to have been sufficiently realised and taken into account. Designers in the wholesale trade are slowly evolving a series of methods whereby much of the shape that was previously obtained only by means of the needle and the iron, is produced by a judicious use of the seam and/or the wedge. It is not suggested that some of these methods were not used by bespoke cutters, but it is claimed that all known means of getting the effects of manipulation are being increasingly adopted under a sectional system of manufacture.

A few simple examples will suggest to the senior student lines along which he may apply the ideas set forth.

(1) In early days methods of creating shape in a vest front were learned. In those cases where breast shape was required it was obtained by cutting from the bottom edge to a point immediately below the breast prominence. The pattern was then folded over the required amount at the front of scye, or in the neck opening, or in both. Thus, although the seam under the bust was the only visible sign, shape had been created by two invisible suppressions, and, if desired, by the breast dart as well.

(2) Subsequently the use of the "Donlon" wedge, removed from the hem of jacket or over-garment in cases of corpulency, would be known. By means of folding over the amount to be removed, the hem was reduced without introducing a special seam for the purpose.

(3) Closely allied with this method is that employed for producing the "barrel hip" effect in a lounge jacket. By folding over a normal pattern from zero at the end of the side dart to the required amount at the hem, the desired "barrel" line was produced. This method secures some of the advantages of a lounge cut with a side-body.

(4) Another use of the wedge in creating local shape is shown in the practice of a firm making up 10-12 oz. tropical suitings. The nature of the materials used prevented them "holding in" the front edge, as they would a heavier fabric. In this case the under-arm dart was cut, and the pocket as far as the front tack. From nil at this point a wedge of 3/4 in. was removed from the front edge. The front edge of the pattern was then slightly re-shaped to meet the alteration.

These examples deal with *the creation of local shape without a local seam.* Other instances will occur to the student. One example of using a seam to create local shape where normally no seam would appear should be given.

(5) In his later system for body coats, Holding used a short dart in the skirt rather than use more than a small amount of fullness. The short skirt-dart coincided with the

side seam of the garment and appeared to be a continuation of it.

The Shoulder.

Any instruction as to methods for shaping a coat shoulder will take into account the shape requirements of the breast.

If the same methods were applied to the shoulders of two coats, and in one of them the breast shape was further emphasised by an under-breast dart, two different effects would be produced. Naturally, the particular effect desired must be clearly in mind before any attempt to secure such shape is made.

The effect generally desired is to produce in the breast and shoulder the convex shape of the figure in the upper thorax.

To do this successfully the length *CD* (Fig. 8) must be maintained at its maximum, while *EF* is shortened and *AB* is kept at a constant dimension by holding fairly and avoiding stretching. If these things are done, then the convexity of the part will have been secured.

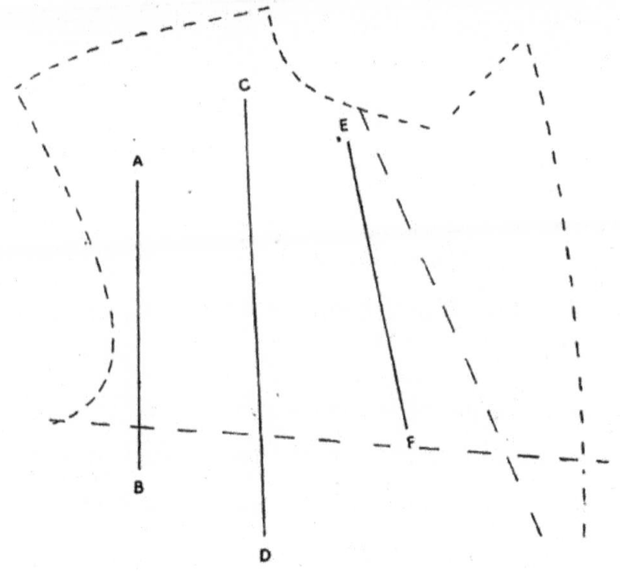

FIG. 8.

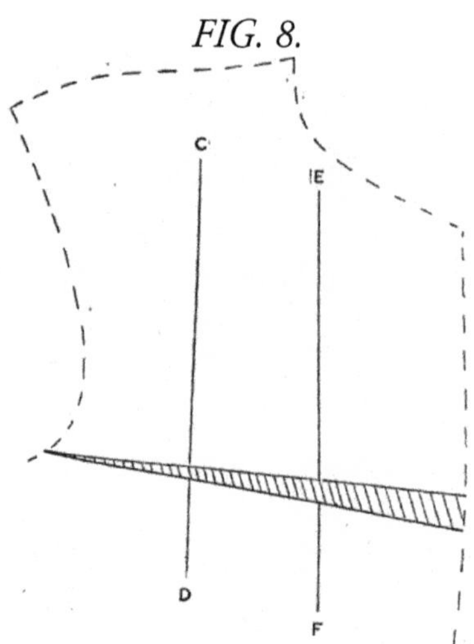

FIG. 9.

In the first place (Fig. 9) it is not desirable to reduce *CD* in any way. This rules out the method of taking out a wedge on, or about, the breast level. Whatever may be the merits of that device in producing a "forward" front, it certainly takes length from line *CD*.

To argue that it shortens line *EF* by a greater amount, and, therefore, *CD* is *relatively* lengthened, evades the issue entirely. The effect of convexity can only be properly obtained if *CD* is maintained and *EF* shortened.

The methods of securing this shape are: (*a*) the dart in the gorge running towards the breast prominence and (*b*) the putting on of a tight bridle. A combination of both methods, in a partial degree, will be found advantageous. Any drastic application of methods (*a*) or (*b*) will result in a too great localisation of shape.

For the normal figure it is suggested, where a breast dart is used in combination, that a neck dart of merely two sewn seams without removing any material, with a 5/8-in. shortening of the crease row by bridling (assuming a lapel of medium length) will give all the shape required in all but special cases.

Forwarding and lowering the neck point will do two things:—

(*a*) pick up the front—*i.e.*, shorten the front balance length, and (*b*) ease the front of scye. It will not, however, of itself give shape: that can only be done locally by means of the gorge dart and by bridling, or by both.

Where the front of scye is desired to fit very closely and the neck-point has been receded (*i.e.*, the shoulder crookened) to effect this, then it is probable that the gorge dart and the bridle will, between them, have to produce a degree of shape greater than usual.

The Back Shoulder.

The back-shoulder section presents in the great majority of cases a greater convexity of surface than the front shoulder. The shapeliness is required between the top (or ridge) of the shoulder downwards over the blade. The problem here again is to treat a flat piece of material so that it will fit a surface not flat. If a dummy figure is taken and a piece of material representing half the back is arranged on it in correct position, the problem will become evident. The half back should be fastened with drawing-pins down the centre from the nape to the breast level. The back neck-point should next be secured, then the top of side seam, lastly the shoulder end. The amount of excess material between the neck point and the shoulder end will vary with the figure. In an erect man with flat blades there will be less; in the round-back figure there will be more. The amount will vary with the degree of shape to be obtained.

In a "regular" figure the nape point will be *about* 2 1/2 ins. from a vertical line taken up from the spine on the breast level (Fig. 10).

For this form type f in. should be added to the back shoulder length.

For every extra 1/4 in. over this amount of 2 1/2 ins. from the vertical, 1/4 in. should be added to the length of the back shoulder.

Thus:—

Nape 2 1/2 ins. from vertical, plus 3/4 in. on back shoulder.

Nape 2 3/4 ins. from vertical, plus 5/8 in. on back shoulder.

Nape 2 3 ins. from vertical, plus 7/8 in. on back shoulder.

The amount eased on the shoulder should first be allowed on the top of the back.

The amount of the excess should be localised by notches placed 1 in. from shoulder end and 1 1/2 ins. from neck. Between these notches the excess of back over front should be eased on.

The above method assumed the "regular" figure, in which the back-seam of the garment will run straight from back breast to nape.

In figures where the head is forward, the garment back-seam should be run in 1/4 in. at the nape. The ability to do this will depend on the pattern of the material. In this respect it will be obvious that the run of *any* seam will have regard to the fabric pattern being dealt with.

The shaping of. the back shoulder by this method will not be restricted to any particular form type. While more is obviously required in any figure with excessive blade development or thick shoulders, it is evident that the posture of the figure is the chief determinant.

A secondary effect of this procedure will be the clearing from the back scye of any excess material.

After several experiments in this method as applied to various form types, the student should note the essential similarity between this method and the creation of shape by means of a panel seam in either a waistcoat back or a costume jacket with the panel arrangement of seams.

Suppressions and Increments.

A suppression is a reduction: an amount removed at a seam.

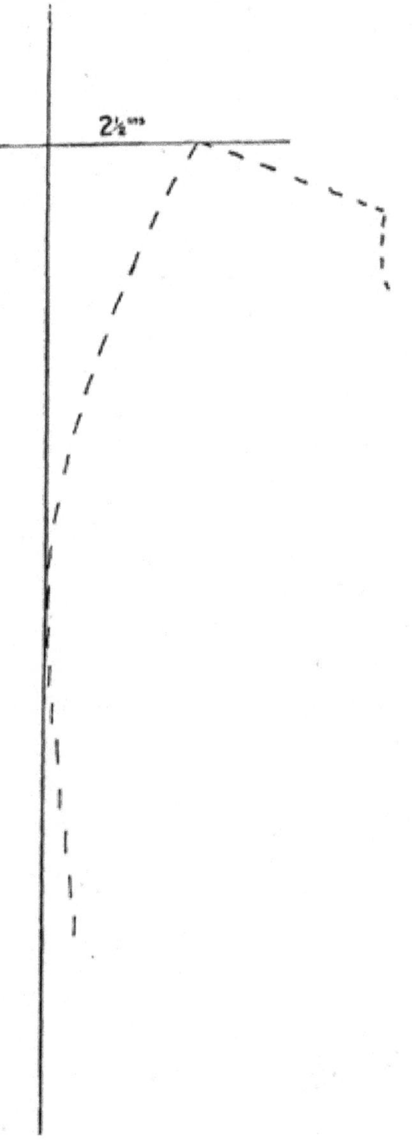

FIG. 10.

An increment is an increase: an amount put in at a seam, generally by overlaying adjacent parts on the flat draft.

In long seams these reductions and additions are made in certain places and on certain seams. The basic principle of shape should be kept in mind: the more shape is required, the more seams there must be. There is a convention, almost a tradition, involved here. In Fig. 7 the vertical seam placement of a representative body coat can be traced. It is first noted that the centre back line is kept quite vertical and straight, no shape being attempted. The centre-front cannot offer any opportunity for shape, for it is never fastened, and its contour is entirely decided by fashion. There can be traced, however, three vertical lines on which shape is secured:—

(1) Beginning at the centre of the shoulder seam, running down over the blade prominence, following the side-body seam, and then down the back pleat to the hem;

(2) From the bottom of the scye, following the side-seam through the waist, then over the eased-on skirt, following the pelvic crown and the hip, to the hem;

(3) From the centre of the shoulder seam, over the breast prominence, following the breast dart, to the hem.

Shape is secured on these three lines: sometimes by a seam, or a seam-equivalent, and sometimes by any form of manipulation. If those three lines are seen in silhouette it will be plain that the shape is there.

To see the perfect example of this, examine the panel arrangement of seams in a lady's jacket. There on those three lines the desired form is created; by means of long seams, running from top to hem of the garment. This arrangement of seams has become a style feature nowadays, but it is actually a necessity of fitting: it is the half-way style between the tight bodice and the sac garment. It is semi-fitting.

The ideal position for fitting seams is, of course, over points of greatest prominence and depression: flat surfaces need no fitting seams. These three fitting lines have, by long usage, become regarded as the lines on which reduction and enlargement shall be made.

Again, where drapery has to be put into a garment, these three lines are again used. Fig. 11 shows the pattern for the back and front of a raglan raincoat. Centre back and centre front are straight, vertical, and shapeless. The hem has to be extended beyond the limits of the flat draft. The problem is, where to infuse the drapery. Centre back and centre front cannot be used, because the back and front must fall straightly to the hem. It would be unwise to put all the drapery into the side seam, by overlaying parts a large amount. The pattern is usually cut up the back from *H* to *F* and *J*: *H* is opened by a few inches, according to the amount of hem-extension required. No extension is made at *F*. A long, thin wedge has been inserted into the back, on the very line it is needed, under the blade. By opening *H* and pivoting on *F*, the back scye is shortened by a little overlapping at *J*. This, if held by a tape before making begins, keeps the drapery in its position. Exactly the same procedure is followed in respect of the front. The increase, or increment, has not been localised in one position, but had been distributed on the three fitting lines.

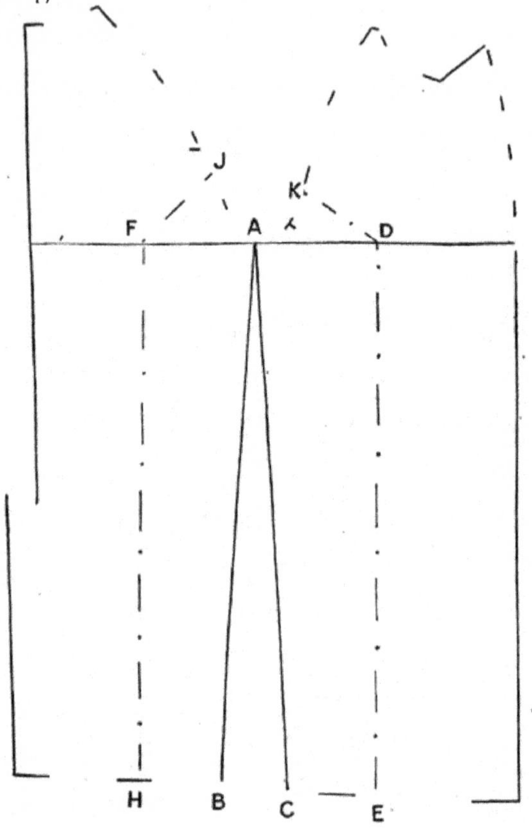

FIG. 11.

Both in suppression and increase these lines should be used. They are traditional in our trade: no one invented them: they were found to answer a need, and were retained as part of the common stock of our craft.

Having agreed *where* to reduce and increase, the *amount* to remove or put in should be discussed. Most pattern systems give definite amounts to be removed or overlaid at the waist, and hip, etc., of long seams. It is very obvious that these given amounts can be correct only for one given figure who has a certain size, and shape, and who stands in a certain way. We get back, then, to the truth that every system-maker has a definite form type in mind when making his system. He will take, say, a 38 regular figure. On the waist line, somewhere between centre back and centre front, two inches of waist suppression must be removed; on the hip line, an inch more or less must be added. To localise the plus and minus quantities is not difficult if the figure is divided up and measured sectionally. Think of the matter, not in terms of the flat two-dimensional pattern, but of the solid three-dimensional figure.

On the breast line of the body, over the waistcoat, put a narrow piece of elastic (1/4 in. wide is recommended) exactly where the tape is placed to take the breast girth, and where the breast construction line appears on the pattern. Then do the same in respect of the waist and seat, taking care to have them parallel to one another and to the floor. The lateral lines are then properly placed.

Next take a vertical rod and place it upright exactly in the centre back. Mark on the lateral elastic bands, by pin or pencil, just where the centre is in each case.

Then do the same at the centre front.

Next place the rod a little to the front of the scye, and mark the three laterals again where they cross.

Finally, do the like close behind the scye (see Figs. 12 and 13).

The trunk of the body is then divided by three lateral lines and four vertical lines.

In this way the suppressions can be made in the appropriate seams:

under the blade, by the side-body seam,
under the arm, by the side seam,
under the breast, by the dart.

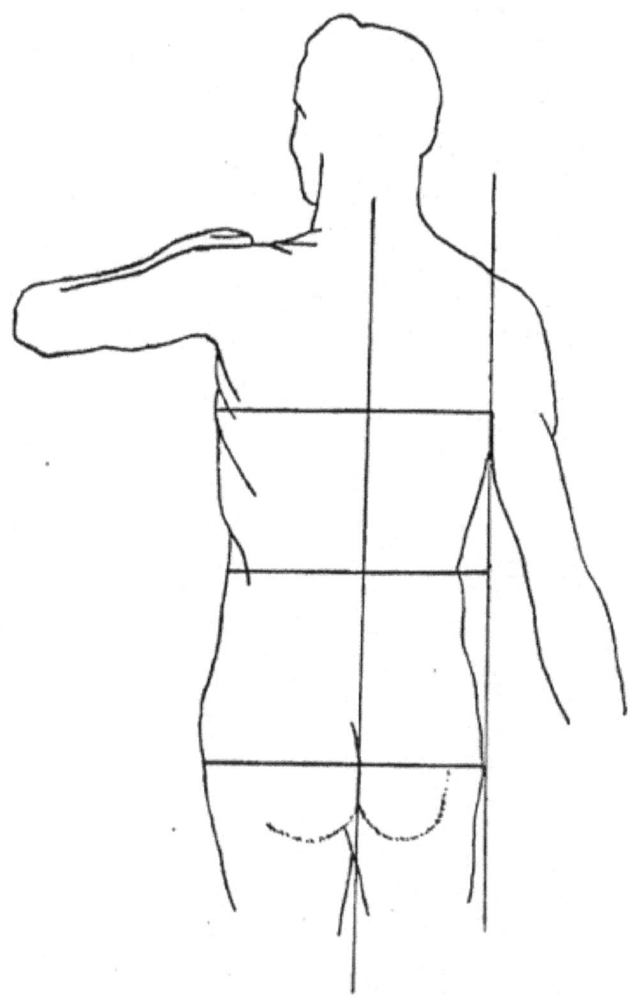

FIG. 12.

(In the lounge jacket the seam arrangement will enable this to be carried out, but not at the same seams. The narrower the back waist, the better the under-blade suppression can be made in the side seam. Then there are the under-arm and breast darts.)

The amounts to be taken out or put in will be decided by measuring each section on the three lateral lines, and by comparing the waist on that line with the breast above. The seat-line sectional measure also should be compared with the breast above. Thus the exact local suppressions and increments can be accurately decided. There is nothing objectionable about this method. The construction lines of the pattern are placed on the body; and the measurements are sectional instead of total. The results may be entered in this form:

	Front.	Side.	Back.	
Breast line . .	6½	5	6½	= 18 ins.
Waist line . .	6¼	4½	5¼	= 16 ins.
Seat line . . .	6½	6	6½	= 19 ins.

This shows that

1/4 in. should be taken out under the breast

1/2 in. should be taken out under the arm.

1 1/4 ins. should be taken out under the arm blade.

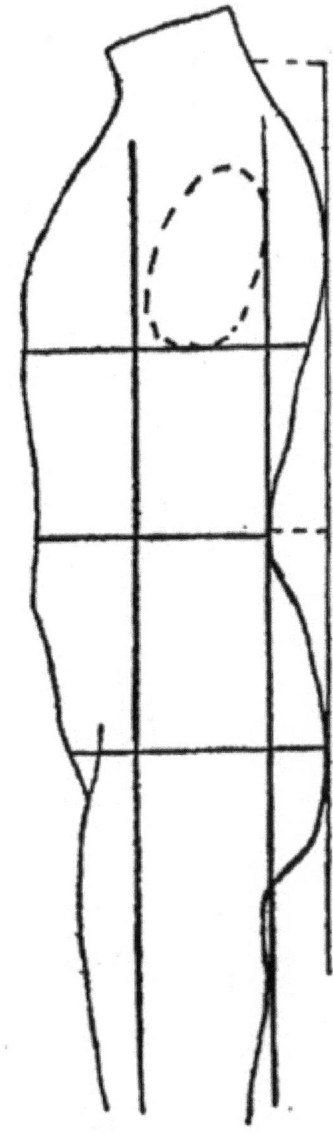

FIG. 13.

1 in. should be added at the side seam or back skirt on the seat line.

This method of sectional measurement is of even greater value when applied to the female figure, with its greater shape values. Particularly, the excess of bust over breast can be correctly measured. An additional lateral line would, of course, be needed for this measure.

The Shoulder Dart.

The forming of a correct shape over the bust and in the gorge, especially in large-girth women, has puzzled many designers. A method is given (Fig. 14) showing how the shoulder dart may be automatically adapted to the size and shape of the figure. Details of construction are given, so that the method may be tested in all sizes.

Breast girth 46 ins.

Bust girth 50 ins.

Scale, 46 + 32 = 78/2 = 39 mean breast girth = 19 1/2 scale.

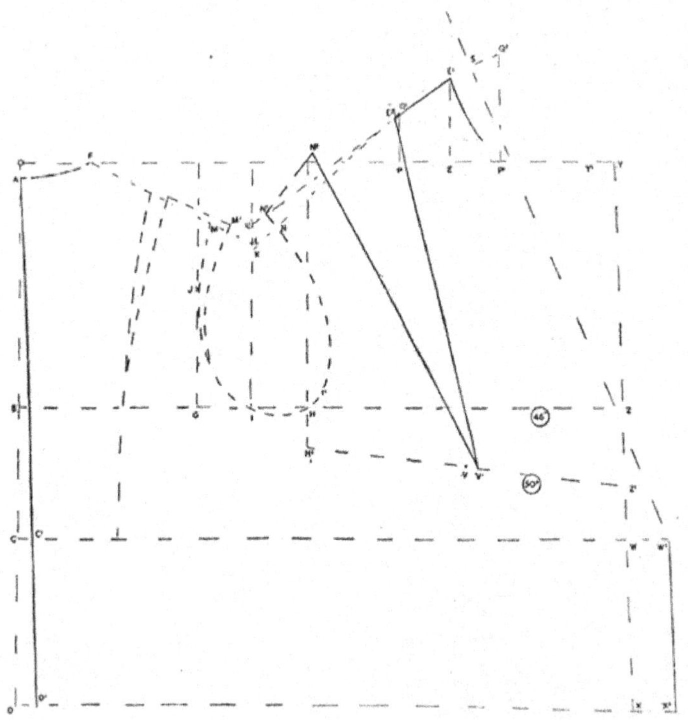

FIG. 14.

OA	= 1/2 in.
AB	= fixed by height and girth.
AC	= nape to waist.
CD	= 7 in.
OF	= 1/6 sc. – 1/4 in.
BG	= 1/3 sc. + 1 in.
BH	= 2/3 sc. – 1/2 in.

I	= midway *GH*.
*CC*1	= 1/2 in.
GJ	= 1/4 sc.
IK	= 1/3 sc.
KL	= 3/4 in.
*C*1 *W D*1*X*}	= 1/2 breast girth, plus half difference between breast and bust, plus 1 in. tolerance = centre front line.
*WW*1	= wrap.
*XX*1}	
M	= 5/8 in. from line *GJ*.
*MM*1	= amount of shape above blade.
*ZZ*1	= 1/6 sc.
HH1	= 1/12 sc.
*YY*1	= 1/24 of half breast in all sizes.
*Y*1*P*1	= 1/6 sc. + 1/2 in.

This gives a line on which the neck point for a garment without a neck dart would be placed: say a coat-frock.

Front-scye line to *P* = 1/6 se. + 1/2 in.

PQ[1] = 3/4 in. constant, + 1/8 in. for every inch of increase of bust above 36 ins.

On this line the neck-point of a jacket for 38 in. breast, or less, and having a normal neck dart, would be placed.

*LL*1 = half the amount *PQ*1 is raised for increase of bust girth.

E is midway *PP*1.

Pivotting at *Z*1 sweep from *Q*1 through *E*1 to Q2.

*E*1 is now the neck point.

(Amount EP^1 should be removed as a neck dart, thus giving greater shape above bust. The shoulder dart and the neck dart together form the amount of above-bust suppression. If either is increased or reduced in quantity, a corresponding compensation must be made in the other. The neck point becomes an arbitrary point fixed with this consideration in mind.)

*E*1*S* = collar stand.

V is midway *H*1*Z*1.

*VV*1 = 1 in. (an arbitrary point).

*E*1*E*2 = half back-shoulder seam length.

*JN*1 = 1/6 sc. + 1 in.

(This fixes the shoulder end; the quantity was ascertained from a JF-size draft of a jacket for a normal figure.) This 1/6 sc. + 1 in. is constant in all sizes.

*N*1*N*2 = half back-shoulder seam length.

N^2E^2 = amount automatically left to be removed as shoulder dart.

The value of this method, which is quite simple when grasped, lies in the fact that it automatically gives the right suppressions for any form type: in the smaller girths a small dart, and in the out-sizes an adequate dart, whatever the form and dimensions. The method is possible only because the shoulder is entirely constructed by scale quantities, while the girths are, of course, direct measurements.

Acknowledgment should be made to Mr. Cleal, of Bourne and Hollingsworth, who was the originator of the method.

Shape in Leg Garments

Provision for Seat.

In the normal regular, figure the front of the body from the waist to hip can be draped with a flat vertical surface of appropriate size. The back of this section, however, cannot be treated in the same way. Firstly, the size and shape of the back of the pelvic region are different: the mass of the gluteal muscles gives a greater contour length. This demands a greater length of garment at this part, compared with the front. Secondly, the normal movement of the lumbar region is forward; any allowance in the garment to allow of this movement must therefore be made at the back.

In constructing the underside of leg garments the top side is used as a basis. The underside is the topside plus:—

(*a*) provision for seat;

(*b*) seam allowance; and possibly

(*c*) extra stride room at the fork.

Provision for the size, shape and movement of the seat muscles is made by constructing the under-side on the assumption that a wedge of material has been inserted. The base of this triangular wedge will be the seat line, about one-sixth of scale above the fork line. The value of the angle will, of course, decide the size of the wedge of material.

For the practical purposes of construction, however, the amount of wedge inserted is indicated by the angle formed by the base line of the fork and the seat closing seam. This angle will: (1) be less acute to provide for garments for more formal wear and (2) more acute to ensure greater ease. These may be known as (1) straighter or (2) more crooked seat angles.

The size of the wedge, by which the under-side exceeds the topside, will depend on several factors. The mass of the seat muscles is one of these factors. While, laterally, this is automatically taken into account by basing the constructional scale on the seat girth and on the application of the direct seat measurement, any unusual vertical requirement must be specially provided for by increased seat angle. The following needs must also be met:—

the attitude of the body;

the ease requirements for bending or stooping;

the appearance of the back of the garment;

the flatness, or otherwise, of the seat.

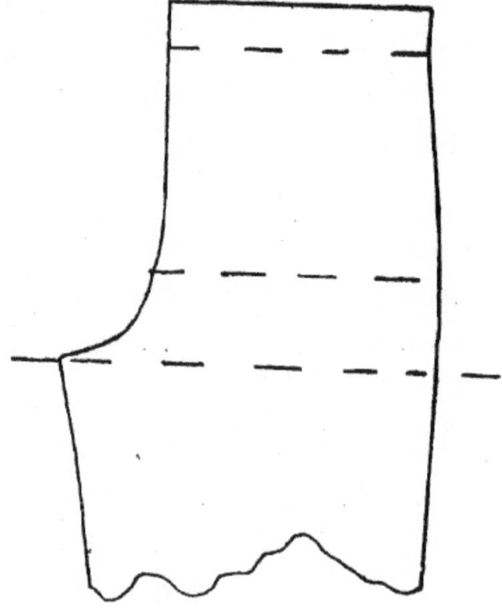

FIG. 15.

Fig. 15 is the topside (body) of a leg garment.

Fig. 16 shows the top-side cut across on the seat line (say 1/6th sc. above fork) and a wedge of material inserted to permit of the extra contour length and allowance for movement being adequately provided for. *This amount will vary from an angle of about* 15 *degrees to one of* 25 *degrees, dependent on the requirements of size, fitting and posture.*

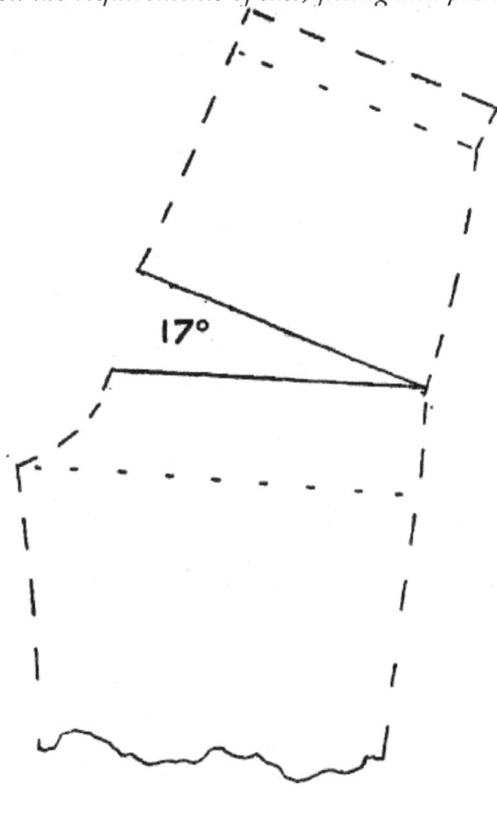

FIG. 16.

Fig. 17 completes the movement begun in Fig. 16 by providing for the shaping of the underside at the back, top and side.

Fig. 18 shows three variations of seat provision in a normal garment. *B* will give a reasonably clean appearance when the wearer stands erect and reasonable ease when sitting. *A* would give a little less easiness when sitting, but would be cleaner in fit in the standing position. *C* would be an appropriate slope of seat seam for working garments or for riding garments.

Lateral Provision.

Fig. 19 shows an arrangement of almost vertical seat seam where a "curtain back" is required. The method effects a clearance of any excess of lateral material by drastically curving the seat seam from fork to seat. The method of removing any seat surplus applies particularly to those garments (such as plus fours and pleated-top trousers, etc.) into which extra seat girth has been introduced for style purposes.

Fig. 20 illustrates the reverse effect by arranging for a seat seam almost straight from fork to waist. This method will secure the extra amount of lateral seat provision necessary in riding garments, where the saddle position demands both vertical *and* lateral provision for seat and posture.

The principle of seat angle may be applied to a garment draft by various methods, all equally good. Once the principle has been grasped, the method or system by which it is applied is secondary. The following method is simple and effective:—

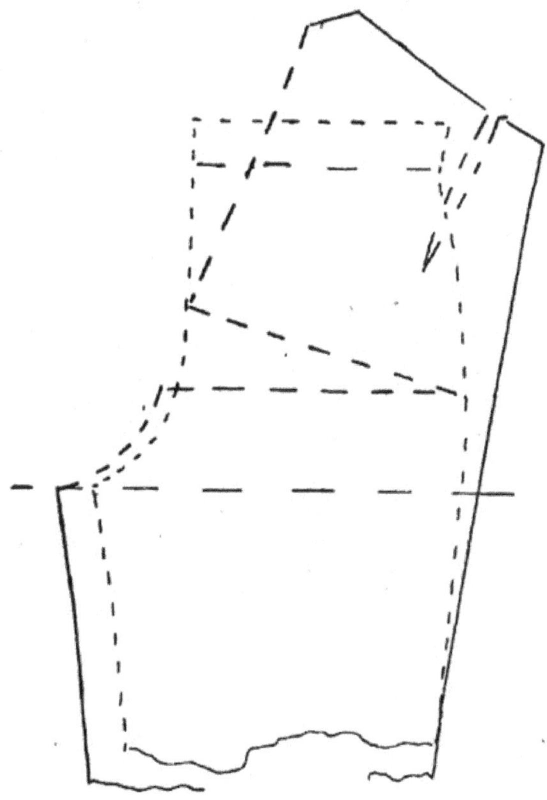

FIG. 17.

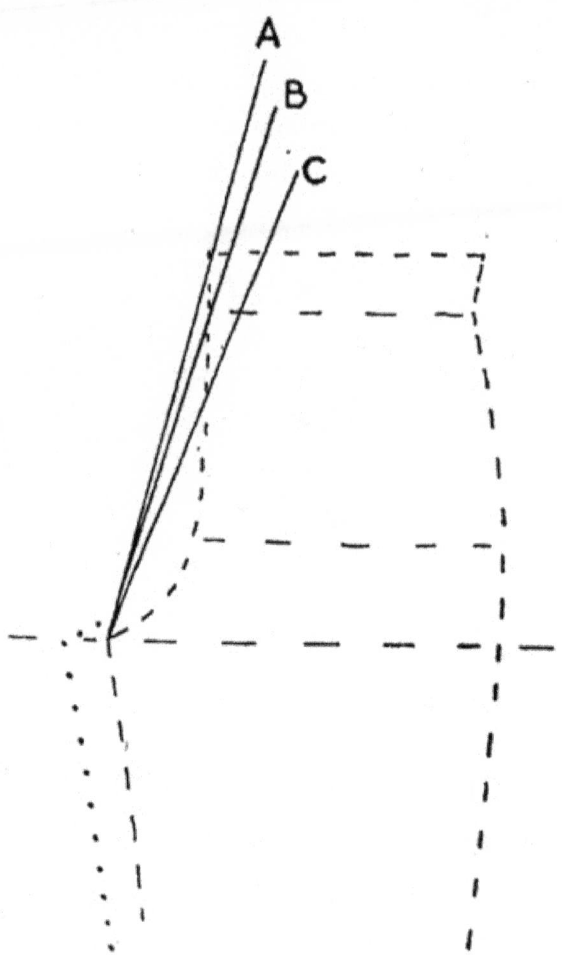

FIG. 18.

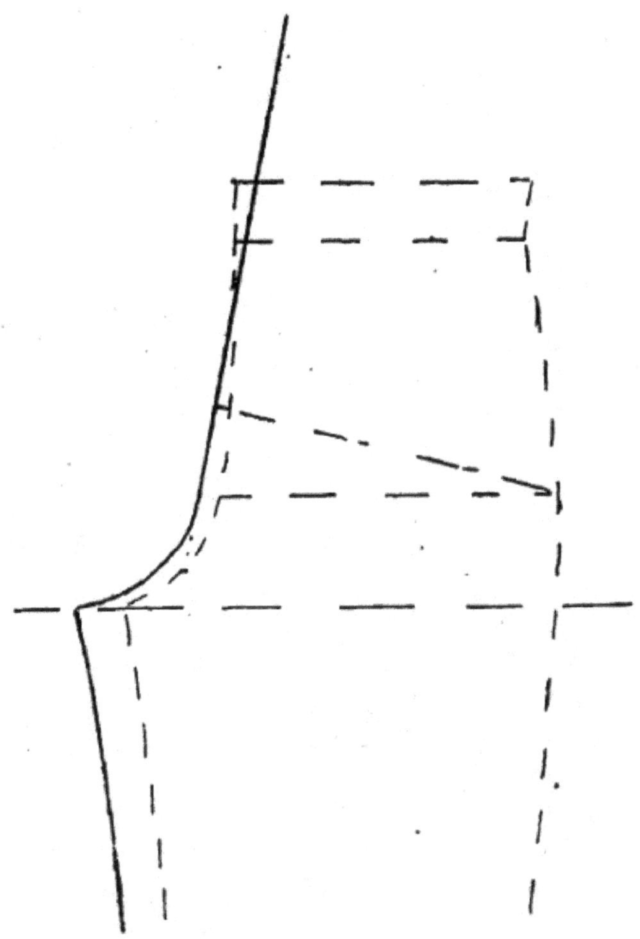

FIG. 19.

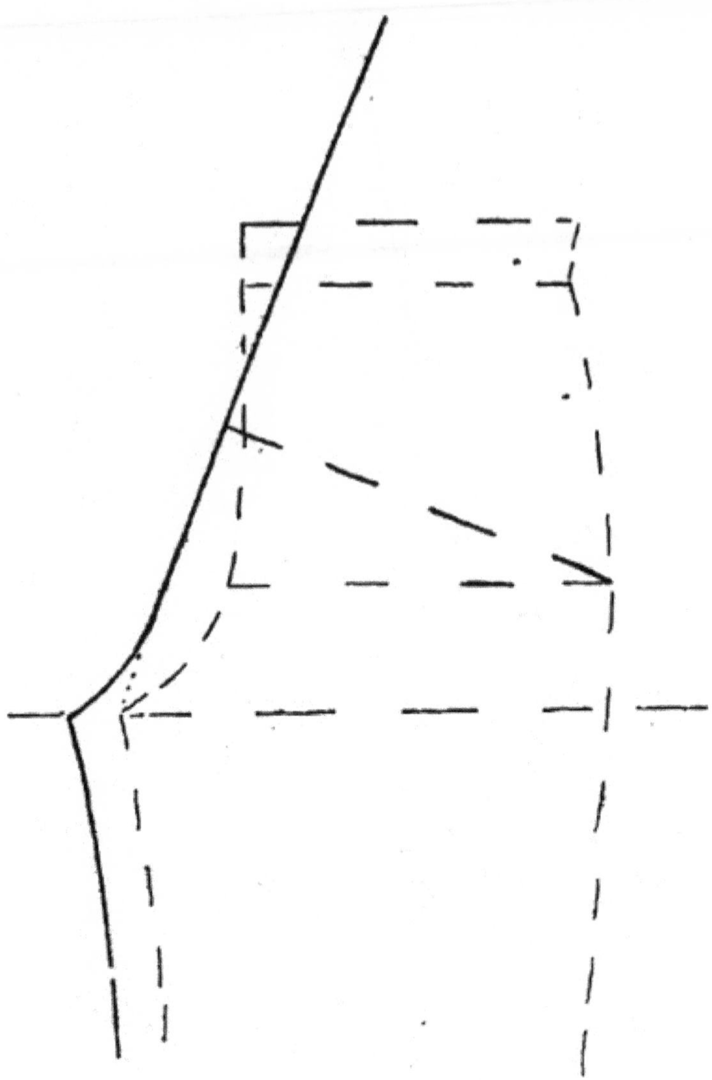

FIG. 20.

Formulæ, for the normal form,

(*a*) Close-fitting, 1/2 sc. + 1 in. up from fork line.

(*b*) Medium fitting, 1/2 sc. – 1/2 in. up from fork line.

(*c*) Easy fitting, 1.3 sc. + 3/4 in. up from fork line.

(*a*) will give seat angle of 15 degrees.

(*b*) will give seat angle of 19 degrees.

(*c*) will give seat angle of 25 degrees.

Intermediate effects may, of course, be obtained by using intermediate quantities.

A flat seat demands a relatively straight seam, while a prominent seat will need a maximum seat angle.

For leg garments for the corpulent figure, assume that the figure is erect in posture, and, therefore, the seat flat. A minimum seat angle will thus be sufficient.

The student is urged to construct his pattern for the underside by using a protractor to give the angle of seat required. This would take him back to first principles, and away from the empirical methods, now in use, which obscure the very principle they seek to apply.

Angle of Seat in the Skirt.

The similarity between the upper parts (fork to waist) of trousers and skirt has been recognised by designers. Fig. 21 shows the front and back of a simple two-piece skirt. In broken lines have been added the amounts of inside-thigh drapery needed to bifurcate the skirt into trousers. In men's leg garments these amounts are called fork quantity and stride room. (Actually they are one quantity divided into two parts by the leg seam.)

In the skirt, the angle of seat *A, B, C* gives the extra length needed for the contour of the seat. In making a skirt pattern this amount is not consciously placed in its actual position by the designer: nor does the system by which the pattern is drawn speak of seat angle. *In the skirt, as in the trousers, the angle of seat is put into the pattern by obscure and indirect means.* The system may, or may not, speak of a "factor of balance", which in the diagram is *KM*. This is the alias or disguise under which provision for seat, in the skirt, masquerades.

The fact is, the underside of a skirt is like the underside of trousers: it must be longer in the centre back line, from seat to waist, in order to provide seat room, and this extra quantity is seat angle.

The industry will one day produce a man who will make a synthesis of all our fitting formulae, now scattered and unrelated in the many systems, which too often confuse the very principles they would make plain. The division of form-fitting into men's systems and women's systems has led many to believe that differences between the male trunk and the female torso lie in more than size and shape. In the interests of clear thinking this is to be regretted.

Waist Suppression (Men)

In the proportionate figure of normal development the waist girth bears a certain relation to the seat girth. For example, a waist measurement of 32 ins. should normally connote a 37-in. seat girth. The table of proportionate sizes will show many similar examples. The range of men's regular, long, and short sizes will show differences between the two measurements of 6 1/2 ins. to 3 ins., according to size. The *size* of the seat and the waist are, of course, transferred to the garment pattern in the way all direct measurements are applied. The *shape*, however, demanded in the seat-waist region can only be secured in the way that all shape is created—namely, by use of correctly-placed seams. The side seam is shaped to fit snugly into the side waist: the top of the seat seam, too, is so shaped that the garment will fit into the hollow of the back without crease or strain. The seat seam is often left open for 1 1/2 ins. from the top.

Shape, however, is required between the side and centre back, so a seam in the form of a dart is placed almost centrally between the two. The axiom here applied is one that holds good in the shaping of all garment parts: "the function of the seam is to create shape; and the greater the amount of shape required, the greater must be the number of seams employed."

(*a*) Where the difference between waist and seat is not more than 6 ins., one dart will be sufficient to provide the shape required in the region.

(*b*) When the difference is more than 6 ins., then two darts will be necessary to properly distribute the abnormal suppression. The two darts should be evenly spaced between the side seam and centre back.

(*c*) In the very few cases where flat seat or insufficiently developed gluteal muscles give a difference of only 2 ins. or 2 1/2 ins. between the two measurements, the dart may be dispensed with entirely.

Whatever amount is required to be removed by darts must first be added, *plus seams*, to the waist measurement as applied to the pattern.

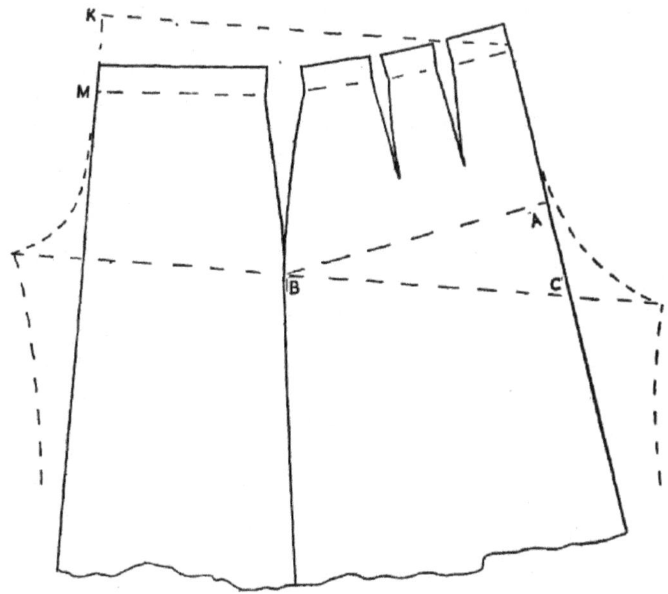

FIG. 21.

The maximum suppression will be made on the waist line, below which the dart will be tapered until it stops short just above the seat prominence. While the length of the dart will naturally vary with the height of the man, and therefore no *exact quantity* can be given, it is seldom that it should extend to a point more than 5 1/2 ins. *below the waist line.*

In trousers having no waist-band the dart will, of course, run through into the top of the trousers. In this case the dart will be slightly decreased *above* the waist line to harmonise with the shape of the body at that part.

The Shape and Finish of Trousers Hem.

Plain bottoms. It should be accepted as a general rule that the length of the trousers leg is related to its width.

The back and sides may fall unimpeded over the heel. The front of the hem, however, rests on the arched instep of the boot. The front of the hem, therefore, must be so shaped as to be farther from the ground than are the back and the sides.

An upturn of from 1 1/2 ins. to 2 ins. is added. When this comes to be turned up during making, the top edge of the front upturn will be found too tight to lie fairly on the top-side. This is generally overcome by cutting down into the upturn at the centre front and inserting an adequate wedge of material.

At the centre of the underside upturn there will be a corresponding amount of excess material. This can quite easily be disposed of when pressing the hem.

The above instructions for shaping a plain hem should, however, be modified by the fact that it is regarded as a desirable style-feature by many tailors for the front of the garment to "break" gracefully above the instep. Where this feature is desired the curve of the front hem will be less pronounced.

The Cuffed Hem (P.T.U.)

Rather different conditions govern the cuffed hem. In the shaped hem the bottom line was irregular, and the main concern was to relate the hem to the shape of the boot.

In the cuffed hem the hem-line must run parallel to the ground; and, this being so, the length of the garment leg is decided by the point at the centre front where the trousers leg meets the shoe.

In the case of narrower leg widths that point will be higher on the instep; and in wider trousers it will be at a lower point, merely by reason of the extra width. For example, a pair of ultra- "Oxford bags " would need to be cut longer, because of the "spread" of hem, than a pair of normal trousers for business wear. Although an extreme example, this comparison will point the obvious relationship between leg length and width.

The following formula will be found useful in calculating the length of leg for any given width:—

Assume that the measurement for plain bottoms has been taken, from the fork to 1 in. above the heel seam of the shoe.

For cuffed hems:

Width			
Width	18 ins.	minus	1½ ins.
„	19 ins.	„	1¼ in.
„	20 ins.	„	1 in.
„	21 ins.	„	¾ in.
„	22 ins.	„	½ in.
„	23 ins.	„	¼ in.
	24 ins. or over		as measure taken.

Example.

Assume an inside leg measure of 31 1/2 ins. and a hem width of 21 ins. Then 31 1/2 ins. — 3/4 in. = 30 3/4 ins., which will be the *net* leg length.

The cuff will normally be 2 ins. deep; so that over the 30 3/4 ins. *net* leg length there will be allowed twice 2 ins. for the cuff = 4 ins. and 3/4 in. for the amount of the upturn. 30 3/4 ins. + 4 ins. + 3/4 in. = 35 1/2 ins. = total length of leg as marked on the pattern.

"Bell Bottom" Trousers.

The abnormal width of the hem (which is the distinguishing feature of this type), and the fitting of the front hem over the boot, will make it necessary for the front to be rounded so as to fall into its correct position on the foot. The method of obtaining a correct shape on the front is to pivot on the centre knee point and describe an arc from side to side. By doing this, the amount of curve on the front hem is automatically harmonised with the width of the hem, whatever may be its size.

Pleated Tops in Trousers.

A comparison of quite recent trousers types with those generally worn, say, twenty-five years ago, will reveal many minor modifications in fashion. But in one important respect the change has been radical. The fashionable trousers of thirty-five years ago made a bold bid at shape. By shrinking under the ham, "easing-on" over the calf and shrinking out over the boot, an attempt was made to follow the general contour of the leg. A "dead" crease at back and front was not then considered desirable.

Today, however, instead of the curved contours, we aim at straight lines. Trousers, today, must obscure, not reveal, the natural lines of the leg. The knee-girth measurement has become almost redundant, and the effect generally attempted is that of slightly tapering lines from the hip to the hem. *But the lines must be straight.*

Curved lines have deserted these leg garments, and have found sanctuary in the lounge jacket, which, in the same period, has lost its box-like aspect and taken unto itself the more gracious curve. So long as a pair of trousers will fit the trouser-press by night, we make no complaint that they merely "drape" ourselves by day.

Pleats are, essentially, suppressions, and the only justification for their use lies in the fact that they produce a certain shape of trousers front—namely, a closely-fitting waist-band with an easiness of fit in the fork and front of thigh. The term "peg tops" suggests the shape produced.

The amount taken up in pleating must first be added to the width of the topside at the waist. Whatever the amount, it must be divided equally between the front and the side: it would be quite wrong to add the total amount at either the side or the front.

Pleating at the waist raises a further related constructional point: were pleats introduced, and no addition made to the hip-girth of the garment, a comparative tightness would be evident at the front of thigh and at the fork. Further, the waist and seat being out of phase, the desired style effect would not be effected. An amount is, therefore, added to the width of each top-side on the fork line, and 1 in. is a quite usual quantity: half of this amount is added at the front fly line and half at the side seam.

Each top-side is thus increased in width on the fork line by 1 in. This quantity is automatically reproduced on the under-sides, seeing that they are constructed on the basis of the top-sides. A surplus of 4 ins. in the total hip-girth will, therefore, result, some part of which would, unless rectified, form unsightly folds at the seat. To avoid this the seat seam is "straightened"—i.e., a minimum of seat angle is allowed; and rather more than the normal amount is removed when curving the lower part of the seat seam.

One or two pleats may be placed at the front waist. The amount allowed to each pleat will depend on the style of garment required and the kind of material used. The pleat, in size, should not be too small: a mimimum of 1 1/2 ins. (*i.e.*, 3/4 in. on the fold) should be maintained. The amount may be increased to 2 ins. with advantage.

It is customary for the edge of the pleat to fold towards the front of the garment. It is also usual for the pleat edge to form a part of the front crease which runs from the waist to hem. This localises the position of the pleat at a point on the waist seam two-thirds of the net top-side width from the side-seam.

Where two pleats are required, they will be evenly spaced on the topside—*i.e.*, equidistant from each other and from the front and side. In this case the long front crease would emerge from the front pleat.

Pleats will not normally be introduced into leg garments for corpulent men.

Leg Construction. Close, Normal and Open Construction.

The normal system of trousers construction assumed that the legs are in a certain position relative to the trunk of the body; that the wearer of the trousers stands in a normal position, the feet not too close together or too far apart.

There are, however, certain garments and certain ways in which men stand, for which special provision must be made.

The corpulent man usually stands with his feet farther apart than does the figure of proportionate dimensions. This is an involuntary change of stance to maintain the better balance and movement of a body, which in bulk has outgrown the legs, which are, of course, the natural support of the trunk. This is an example of the necessity of a more open leg construction for an altered stance.

Garments worn mainly for horse-riding, too, demand an openness of leg construction, to ensure comfort in the saddle position. This is an illustration of the need for a very open leg construction to provide for a special position in wear.

Now, in these two instances the garment legs have been opened for certain sufficient reasons. The differences between these garments and those of normal construction should be noted:—

(*a*) the distance from fork to knee has been increased,

(*b*) the inside leg seam has been lengthened,

(*c*) the side seam has been shortened.

If a pair of leg garments cut with an open leg were placed on a man who stood in the normal way, surplus material would be noticeable in the fork. This would, of course, be regarded as an undesirable happening.

On the other hand, it will be seen that, while openness of leg construction increases the distance from fork to knee and gives an excess of inside leg length around the fork, the opposite—*i.e.*, closeness of leg construction—would give less inside leg length, and consequently no surplus or excessive material in the fork.

Therefore, if trousers are to be constructed for either a man who stands with feet closer than the normal, or for wear where a close fork fit is demanded (*e.g.*, dress kit), the method of close construction should be adopted.

The legs of trousers should be varied from the normal if the position of the legs relative to the trunk, or the special requirements of wear, appear to demand such alteration.

In work garments, too, a more easy fitting may be obtained by a slight openness of cut.

The movement of the centre leg construction line in the direction of the side-seam should not normally exceed 3/4 in., and in the opposite direction by more than 1/2 in.

THE DESIGNING OF SPECIALITY GARMENTS

THE student will be called upon, during his working life, to design patterns of many garments that are outside the normal types of civilian clothing. These special garments fall into fairly distinct groups; each garment within a given group possessing the main characteristics of the group to which it belongs.

These garments may be regarded as an index of the times in which they were most popular, and reflect the rise and passing of definite phases of social life. The term "livery" has meant different things at various times. All social changes carry with them sartorial consequences, and the student of clothing should realise the significance of the infinitely greater demand for commissionaires' uniform than for, say, footmen's livery garments. The general adoption of the internal-combustion engine, and the consequent decline in the number of horse-drawn vehicles, has resulted in a radical change in the kinds of livery worn. The chauffeur's driving coat has almost displaced the box coat of the coachman.

The number of male servants, indoor and outdoor, has declined rapidly and considerably during the last thirty years: the butler's pantry jacket and the gamekeeper's coat are less frequent today. With this decline in the number of male servants has gone a corresponding great increase in the number of large residential hotels maintaining a uniform staff of men servants.

The playing of games and the almost universal personal participation in outdoor sports, which is one of the healthy characteristics of recent years, have resulted in the production of a wide range of garments particularly adapted to the ends of outdoor activity. Golf, tennis and "hiking" have each evolved a group of garments specially suited to their own sartorial needs.

It is not maintained that there is a wider range of garment types worn today than in pre-war, or even pre-motor days: it is quite probable that the variety is not nearly so wide now as then. But it is certain that new occasions do, of necessity, produce new garment types, and it is equally certain that the terms "livery" and "special garment" will mean something different to the modern student than to his predecessor a generation ago.

Further, the changes enumerated above are merely a sketchy illustration, confined to one generation, of the evolution of dress that has accompanied the general social evolution of civilised man. While these changes are hardly perceptible from season to season and from year to year, yet, looking back over a number of years, it is possible to estimate these changes and to note that dress has been progressively adapted to the wider needs of life, while retaining its sense of artistic values.

At the same time, changes have taken place in the methods of garment production: the specialist has emerged to deal with special garment types. In the old retail bespoke business it was possible to find the all-round man, capable of producing a very wide range of garments, but even then firms, through a long and successful experience of certain special types, became specialists in clerical, military or livery garments. Within the factory organisation of the industry today are found specialist firms who confine their activities to certain types of garments and who do those specialities extremely well.

In this special branch of the industry, then, dealing with specialised productions along lines different from those of the more normal methods, lie opportunities for advancement and interesting work. A bulky volume would be necessary to deal adequately with the distinctive design, the materials and the style features of the large number of speciality garments in current use. The trade technical Press, in book form and in periodical journals, deals from time to time with many of these garments, but no comprehensive up-to-date text-book on special garments can be recommended. It will, however, be found that the three following considerations will give the student an orderly approach to a branch of the industry that demands more than average ability and technical knowledge.

(1) Fabric.—The first notable feature of every group of special garments is that certain materials are very closely identified with distinctive garments. While this is true, to a limited extent, of the more normal garments of everyday civilian wear, it is even more so in respect of speciality wear. For example, to say that a garment is for clerical wear, is to restrict it to neutral colour and a narrow range of materials.

Motor liveries, flying kit, tropical outfits or commissionaires' uniforms, to mention only a few, each imply a restricted variety of fabrics and colours. Just as stable tweeds and pilot cloths used to connote certain definite garments, so do many of the more modern materials suggest the garment into which they will be made.

Changes, of a minor kind, are continually taking place, but the results, taken over a term of years, are considerable. Materials and colours may change most in the newer liveries and uniforms—*e.g.*, cinema attendants. In the older forms of garb, ecclesiastical, legal, civic and academical gowns and robes, and the dress of the livery-men of the great city companies, colours and fabric are almost static.

Certain special garments are lined with materials especially suited to its special use. One may carry a fleece lining, another be lined with cloth. A bulky lining demands a larger coat, and garments of this type require considered additions to size.

(2) Style Features.—Just as there are distinctive fabrics and colours for the various special garments, so there are *style features* which are their distinguishing marks. Many of these features are archaic, they have no modern justification in utility, and are decorative survivals of an earlier day. The hood, the sword-flash and the side-edge are instances. It is well to remember that in all speciality garments *the details are of the first importance:* they must be made to certain definite specifications, or they lose their distinctive character and the garment becomes part of the common stock of normal dress. This point will be apparent if, say, a groom's stable jacket is compared with a normal lounge, or a chauffeur's driving coat with the over-garment of his employer. The great importance of accuracy of detail, then, is obvious. This leads to a consideration of how an accurate knowledge of the details of speciality garments may be obtained. Some branches have been fairly adequately dealt with in technical publications: the dress of livery servants, the clergy; the robes and gowns of academical and ecclesiastical dignitaries. But many sections have not received the special and separate treatment they merit, and the time is perhaps ripe for the issue of a comprehensive volume on speciality garments. In the meantime, the student is advised to collect and file, for his own use, particulars of any garment falling into any special group, which may appear in the trade technical Press. Good illustrations, particularly photographs, showing general and special style features, descriptions in letter-press, notes on colour and materials, trimmings used, and any other matter of special use and interest. In this way he builds up a body of matter on a special subject that will be of use to him as a designer of such garment types. The search for, and collection of, such particulars will, during student days, help to develop the useful faculty of discrimination. Such a collection of selected matter should be preserved in a loose-leaf filing case, properly indexed and kept up-to-date.

(3) The Use of a Base Pattern in Designing Specialities.—It has already been seen that a very wide variety of special garments can be divided into groups, each group possessing distinguishing characteristics. Every garment within a given group will differ in some respects from all others within the same group. But, while it is possible to show the points of difference between them, it is also possible to recognise that *there is a basic similarity between them all.* The points of difference demand that, in certain respects, they must be regarded as individual types; the points of similarity, however, do certainly relate them to a common base. Take as an illustration the large group of garments based on the military frock. This garment is worn by the officers of practically every English regiment, and *basically* it is the same in every case. The various regiments, however, have this garment finished with a very wide variety of style features, enabling the various units to be distinguished by their dress. The illustration may be extended to cover the growing number of uniforms worn by bandsmen, hotel, bank and cinema employees which obviously derive from the military frock.

The military tunic offers an equally good illustration. (See *Dress Regulations for the Army*, H.M. Stationery Office.)

It is, therefore, suggested that the student should, when examining any unfamiliar garment style, look beyond the style features which give it individuality, and endeavour to find the base on which those style features have been superimposed. Once the garment has been placed in its basic group, the work of pattern design has been greatly simplified.

Considered from the lowest standpoint, that of orderly procedure, this method of working up from a base, from the simple to the complex, is to be commended.

With this in mind, special garments that are given as exercises should be chosen with a view to dealing with as large a number of basic styles as possible.

The important matter is to be able to recognise the basic foundation of a garment, and to realise that the style features are something added to that foundation.

Finally, in this direction, it is well to have in mind the values that are contained in the groups of garments we are considering. Every garment combines, in varying and unequal degrees, utility and decoration. It is easy to argue, for example, that in a flying kit the utility of the garment is more obvious than its decorative value. But, on the contrary, it could be maintained that even such a garb, so well adapted to its peculiar use, arouses a feeling of satisfaction and a sense of the fitness of things. It may be said to fit into its environment as easily and as naturally as a half-timbered thatched cottage harmonises with the English scene; and whether it is high art should not be asked, rather, is it good design? In a clothing warehouse it would be merely a glorified overall; in the airplane it is the right thing in the right place, and therefore good. A really good flying kit would, however, be incongruous on a tennis-court or at the Trooping of the Colour: it wouldn't belong.

All speciality garments, whether they be merely utilitarian or purely decorative, or any combination of the two, are designed to meet special needs. The supreme test of any garment, then, is whether it successfully fulfils the ends for which it has been produced. This final note should be read as suggestive of the lines along which garment design should develop.

THE GRADING OF PATTERNS

1. Historical Note.

1820

MR. J. WYATT, one of the earliest writers on Pattern Drawing, published, in his *Tailor's Friendly Instructor*, a plan for developing large-size garment patterns from smaller ones, which he termed "contraction and expansion".

1823

Mr. J. Golding published a method of grading.

Probably owing to the inadequate nature of the information accompanying the diagrams of Wyatt and Golding, the idea did not commend itself to the trade.

A new development came in the nature not of a new method of grading, but in the form of a graduated tape, or set of tapes, which, in their use, embodied the idea of expansion and contraction. The number of units given to find any point or part were maintained constant, but the size of the individual unit varied, but varied regularly, arithmetically, and proportionately.

1890

The next development of the idea was brought out by Mr. D. E. Ryan, an American, who announced that he was prepared to teach "Ryan's garment-grading science", which he called the "missing link ".

2. Methods of Pattern Grading.

(*a*) Grading from one pattern.

(*b*) Grading between two patterns.

(*c*) Grading long, short, and stout sizes from a regular pattern of the same breast girth.

(*d*) Varying from a standard, proportionate pattern for a particular or unusual type of figure.

3. The Principles of Pattern Grading.

To grade a pattern is to enlarge or reduce it in size, while retaining the original form and all the essential style features.

Assume that a trial garment has been produced and passed as correct. The problem is to make patterns of larger or smaller dimensions which will produce garments larger or smaller than the first, but *similar in every respect but size.*

The suggestion that patterns are graded to save time does not appear to be justified. A pattern could be drafted afresh for every new size in less time. The only reason for grading, then, is to secure similarity through a range of sizes.

The best-known authorities on pattern grading are Simons, in America, and Sytner, in England. Koln, of Berlin, and Poole, of Leeds, follow Simons in everything but non-essential details. A study of their principles and methods will show an underlying unity.

First, as to principles: In grading from one pattern and in grading between two patterns, the idea of proportional growth and development is accepted and applied. It is assumed that every enlargement or reduction will be proportionate—*i.e.*, that *lengths and girths* will be affected in correct ratio. Proportionate growth implies that as a form increases in girth there is an increase in height, and vice versa. Only thus can proportion be maintained.

The idea of arithmetical progression is accepted and applied. This assumes that, within the limits of a given form-type, all growth will be distributed in correct ratio. Assume that height is to breast girth as 68 is to 38, any increase in one of these factors implies a proportionate increase in the other factor. Further, if the breast, waist, and seat girths stand to each other in the ratio of as 38 is to 34 is to 40, then any increase or decrease in the dominant factor implies a proportionate increase or decrease in the other factors.

There are two well-recognised exceptions to this principle—namely, (*a*) the grading of a large corpulent size from a smaller corpulent size, and (*b*) the grading of a large X.O.S. from a small O.S. In these cases (*a*) the stomach and (*b*) bust respectively do not develop evenly or proportionately; and thus the idea of arithmetical progression breaks down because uneven deposit of tissue has *produced a different shape.*

No attempt should be made to carry the grading of a pattern beyond the limits of its usefulness. Only patterns of the same form-type should be used in a set of grades. If development and growth were even and equal in height and girth from youth to age, then one may use a boy's pattern as a starting-point for grading patterns for adult and middle-aged figures. The man would have the boy's form-type increased in size only. But the physical characteristics change during life and each stage of growth represents a type; and it is only within the limits of the type that grading is effective.

A regular may be graded from a regular; a stout from a stout; a matron's size from a matron's, etc. But it would be unwise to try to evolve a 44 stout from a 34 regular, or a 42 matron's size from a 34 maid's fitting. There would be no proportionate growth from the smaller to the larger in either case; the respective shapes are quite different; they do not assume the same attitude, therefore the balance of the one will not be correct for the other. The principle of arithmetical progression is not possible of application in any case where general shape, as well as size, changes.

Grading, then, can successfully apply only where size additions or deductions are to be made, but where shape remains unaltered.

The advice "grade often" is to be taken in the sense that it is unwise to attempt to grade out of, or beyond, the figure-type of the original.

The question which is often put in "garment design" question papers, as to whether it would be possible to grade for all sizes from a 26 to a 44 from one pattern, is answered in the above statement of principles.

In grading a long, short, or stout from a regular pattern of the same breast girth, the formulæ given by Simons, *Science of Human Proportions*, and by Popkin, *Production and Technology of Men's Clothing*, should be followed.

Variation from standard pattern for a particular type of figure is not strictly grading in the sense of the three previous methods, but seeing that the alterations made to the basic standard pattern proceed along definite lines and call for exact knowledge of form types, it may be included in this consideration. As an illustration of the method, it may be required to produce a garment which has been very successful for a city type of regular figure, for a regular range suitable for an industrial district.

Here, again, the lines of the garment must be strictly maintained and the style features faithfully copied. The shape of the industrial figure will be "thicker" than the city type, the neck will be a little larger in girth, the shoulder-content greater, and the waist and seat-girths a little in excess. These variations can be measured, and are known in detail; the slight balance adjustments, too, are familiar.

A similar line of argument applies where a pattern for a women's garment for a "provincial" or "industrial" figure has to be produced from a pattern originally designed for a "suburban" type.

The only further advice concerns (a) *accuracy of actual working*. Where so many points are concentrated within a very small area, the importance of fine work will be obvious. All marks and lines should be fine and correctly placed, and all measurements accurate. Tracing, too, calls for accuracy. (b) A really *detailed knowledge of a reliable size-*

chart is essential. One should aim at being able to put down accurate and detailed data, both in measurements and in figure-description, of any size or form-type called for.